# OBAMA, THE DREAMER'S DREAM

## A Memoir

Dr. Eleazar Azuoma Onyeali

iUniverse LLC
Bloomington

**Obama, the Dreamer's Dream**
**A Memoir**

iUniverse books may be ordered through booksellers or by contacting:

iUniverse LLC
1663 Liberty Drive
Bloomington, IN 47403
www.iuniverse.com
1-800-Authors (1-800-288-4677)

ISBN: 978-1-4917-0861-3 (sc)
ISBN: 978-1-4917-0860-6 (e)

Printed in the United States of America.

iUniverse rev. date: 09/28/2013

"Parity suppressed, parity denied.
So many eyes cried, so many hearts wounded
Parity suppressed, parity denied.
So many souls tortured, so many voices silenced
Parity suppressed, parity denied.
So-so many slayed, in the fight. Yet so many, advocate,
Till they died
Parity suppressed, parity denied.
So many tired feet marched and marched and marched,
So-so many just hands roped, maimed, or jailed
Parity suppressed, parity denied.
So many dreams, dreamt, so many dreams, submerged
Parity suppressed, parity denied.
Still many dared to dream, predict, even prophesied
But, pardon me, Obama, a black
man, in the white-house,
President!
Yes sir! Oh yes. America's fairly-spoken. It's Obama!
At last, oh at last, the dreamers' dream.
Parity, redeemed?
Yes indeed. Parity redeemed.
Parity, restored?
At last. Parity restored.
In fairness?
Yes, fair and square, by parity."

"In their times, them young men dreamt big dreams.
In our times, them old men, saw visions."

# Preface

This manuscript was written in two parts and was meant for publication in a local Denver newspaper. The first part, titled "Why Obama Will Be President," was published in the month of August, during the Democratic Convention, in the *Body of Christ News*.

As the general election drew nearer, watching and listening to Barack Obama's "good news and hope" message, I felt more inspired, as if I personally knew this guy. The refreshing, heartwarming message and the grassroots movement Obama is building and spreading across the country, just like a wildfire, I call "The Obama Phenomenon."

It is catching on fast, very unprecedented, and awesome.

I must concede, though, that at the beginning, I was not 100 percent for Obama. I was working mostly on logic then, fashioned by my conscience. My thought was let Clinton be the Democratic nominee for president and Obama her VP.

I was also convinced from the beginning of the election that a Democrat would win the presidency this time around and that Mrs. Clinton would likely beat her Republican opponent by a small margin.

In my heart of hearts, though, I wanted Obama to be the president, but I was nervous. "Is America ready for a president who is black?" I continued to wonder. But being a VP would do for now, I thought, because by my rationale, Obama would mostly be sitting in the backseat and would not be too imposing on white America's psyche. By the end of four years, America would be so used to seeing him at the back stage that his transition to presidency would be less controversial and smoother.

However, when I got to the caucus early this year, Obama's magnetic gravity, even in his absence, pulled me to his side. I switched and voted OBAMA. Yeah!

I left the caucus building that evening with a totally different feeling. Obama has a grounded force, akin to gravity. That he was unstoppable, that he, Barack Obama, was ready to be number two to nobody. After sweeping through the rest of the primaries and finally dismantling the formidable Clinton political machinery, I knew Obama was the one.

Meanwhile, I heard about his book *The Audacity of Hope* and went to the Tattered Bookstore to get a copy. I ended up buying two of his books, including *Dreams from My Father*, which I found more native and much more inspiring.

At the end of the two books, I came to a personal conviction. I concluded that this guy Obama is special, and his movement and call for change, which I call "The Obama Phenomenon," is not an accident or chance event. It is the dreamer's dream come true, right in my lifetime. Obama's whole life, if you ask me, is a book of the times.

I am convinced that this inspiring and infectious phenomenon is Dr. Martin Luther King's "I Have a Dream" speech come true and that Barack Obama himself was the one, the very Negro who Robert F. Kennedy had predicted to be the first black president of the United States of America. The change I believe.

# Acknowledgments

To my eighty-five-year-old mother, whose strength, love, and resilience has more than anything else continued to inspire me.

To all my beloved siblings and cousins, especially Vincent, Ije, and Adaku, who have grown closer to my heart with time.

To my great cousin Professor Ernest Emenyonu, whose literary prowess inspires me to write.

To my wife, who insists that I write.

And to my two children, Ihuoma and Obinna, you give me joy.

# Introduction

My wife and I are completely opposite when it comes to dreaming. Maybe it's the way we sleep. Or maybe it's the very side of the bed we sleep in that affects the way we dream—I'm not so sure. But ever since we got married over twenty years ago (she's the one keeping accurate count), my wife has taken possession of the right side of our bed, as if it were some sort of right in the conjugal agreement, written and signed (by us) apparently, in one of her nightly-dreams—I mean to say in her head. And talking about heads, my wife always sleeps with what I call mountains of pillows piled under her head, leaving me with just one. But that's all right with me. My preferred (sleeping) posture is definitely without much propping. Almost horizontal and always fetal. Yeah.

My wife also has this unusual passion for bright red comfort-warmers lately, which she changes or replaces (with yet a newer red one) right at the beginning of every new season.

"What do you think, babe?" she asked as I walked into our bedroom. She was standing right at the foot of the bed with hands bowed at her hips and wearing her latest Victoria's Secret nightie.

I'd just pulled a thirteen-hour shift, and my vision was somewhat hazy. "About what, that?" I advanced toward her, rubbing on her wares and kissing her on the cheek. "Sure feels sexy babe," I added.

"Not me, silly," she said, pushing my left hand off her thigh. "The new covers." She pointed.

"Oh that? I swallowed some mucus-saliva mix in my throat. "Nice. Real nice."

She hopped back onto the bed and slipped under the red comforter, hugging it. "This feels nmm-nmm soft, babe. I got it from Macys."

Although I prefer she wouldn't be spending too much of our money on new stuff every month, I must concede that the ambient freshness and alluring smell of such nights in our bedroom, especially on the first of the month, puts sparks in my groin and turns the switches on. She relishes the outcome, always. I grant you that. Besides being the nicest husband she married (so I've been told by her close friends), who sees most things in life from a sort of debonair iris, I have never questioned or lost a night's sleep worrying about her little quirks. After all, my wife's comfort (I believe), especially in the bedroom, is ultimately my heart's desire.

Most other nights of the month (especially after a good foofu dinner), I would drag myself upstairs to our bedroom and seconds later, my head and I are evenly aligned on my (designated) side of the bed, all snuggled up under the red comforter, a-sleeping. Yeah, calm and fetal I sleep, just like our (satiated) daughter used to sleep at three months.

My wife, on the other hand (with the exception of the first night of the month), usually comes up an hour or two later, after catching up on late-night movies and stuff. And she prefers to sleep in an almost sixty-degree incline (head-high) on her back, facing the ceiling. Supine position, folks in the medical field call it. Definitely nothing superb about it, if you ask me. Not the most tranquil (sleeping) position to my ears, which would prefer a soothing quietude of night sounds. Thanks to the makers of all them king-sized beds, a dedicated husband (like me), in an effort to preserve all conjugal bedroom courtesy, could once in a while find a distant, safe corner to hide or cover his head and ears and muffle off noxious sounds. I guess some wives would do the same thing too—if not more—should their husbands' noisy snore disrupt their sleep night after night.

Yeah, king-sized beds are really the best way to go, guys, especially if you are married. Even if you're not married, get one. It will make you hunger for a real live partner, especially at midnight—trust me, I've owned four. The first two were in my bachelor years. All waterbeds, hmm-hm. The warm and sometimes wavy feel from that body of water on your skin sort of lifts your soul up into orbit. Celestially awesome. My last two, including that ultra-expensive waterbed that we had for only three months, was as a husband. As good and wonderful as waterbeds are (and yes they are), manufacturers should start to attach a warning label on the side saying, "If your wife is hydrophobic—that is a fear of water (a disease I didn't know if my wife had, because she never complained—or if you have a three-year-old son (that always wants to stick his doggy-nose and tiny little fingers in everything in the house), do not buy a waterbed, queen or king size. Never!

I had a vibrant three-year-old son, dubbed the "inquisitive destroyer" by my baby sister. I love my son to death, but there have been times I thought God or somebody sent me a curse or something.

One Sunday evening, as I sat by my music cabinet trying to figure out why, all of a sudden, the music player stopped working, my sister Ije shouted from the kitchen area, "It's your nosy little son, brother. I've been telling you, you've got the most inquisitive-destroyer for a son, I swear."

I let out a loud puff. My eyelids tightened as I shook my head. "That boy, that naughty little boy's giving me gray hair, I swear." I leaned on my right elbow and with my neck extended backward asked, "God, what's wrong with my boy?"

Ije, who was doing her morning chores in the kitchen, busted out laughing. "Brother, my big brother, Mother said you should never complain a thing about your son."

"Why would Mother say something like that?

"Because according to our mother, and no disrespect big brother, you were worse."

My cheeks bulged with humor, on account of my own baby sister comparing my life at three to my crazy son's. "But you weren't even born then, baby sister. You shouldn't believe everything you hear."

"Are you calling your mother a liar then?"

Oh boy. When it comes to intricate family arguments, as this was turning out to be, my two sibling sisters and my wife sound like they are from the same planet, I swear. They always have a way of deploying their tongue like a jagged saw right at my neck, forcing my back to the wall and destroying my defenses.

"No, baby sister," I replied, and I can feel my eyebrows pulling together at the same time as my head was seeking an escape. "I was just—"

"Brother, please," cut in Ije, "you don't need to say any more." She bent down, scooping some dirt off the kitchen floor. "Mother is always right, and you know that, brother."

She emptied the pan into the big trash can by the sink and said, "I see it all clear, what Mother said about you, right here in my nephew."

Pulling my lips together, I was able to suppress the surging smile inside me.

"Boys are a handful, and that's why I pray to have all girls when I finish school and get married."

"Hey, don't curse yourself baby sister," I said, pulling an electrical cord off the wall socket.

Ije dropped the broom and dustpan on the floor, stood up straight, placed her palms on her hips, and looked up to the roof. "God knows I'm not cursing myself." She then levels her eyes and said, "This is the twentieth century, brother, and girls are deemed as good a blessing today as boys, I grant you that. If not better. Just look at my niece and compare." She clasps her palms atop her chest and adds softly, "She is sweet, calm, and harmless, like an angel."

Well, after what happened two days later, I was inclined more than ever before to swallow most of my Igbo-inherited male dictates (a male-heir-only-world, not unlike the biblical times), and see with less prejudice the new world, at least from my baby sister's point of view.

It was late Tuesday afternoon. Schools had just closed for the year and Ije was home with our kids. My wife and I had gone to work.

"Auntie! Auntie," our seven-year-old daughter screamed from her room, "water, water!"

Ije dropped the rest of the green onion she was chopping in the sink—including the kitchen knife in her left hand—and ran toward the staircase. But it was too late.

Water, like from a broken dam, was roaring and gushing downstairs, flooding the living room and everywhere.

"My God!" she shouted. Looking upstairs and catching the wet and terrified eyes of her nephew (who was quivering on his toes by the hallway, his back plastered to the wall), Ije quickly plodded upstairs as best she could against the heavy flood.

"Come to me, babe," Ije said, sweeping him off his shaky feet. Clenched in his right hand still was the alleged "crime weapon": my wife's scissors, which had probably been lying atop her sewing desk by the bedside.

Turning to my daughter, Ije said, "Run with me, hurry, hurry!" She took them both rushing, into her own room.

She then picked up the phone. "Auntie, Auntie," she panted, "the house is flooded."

"Flooded?" My wife shouted, almost dropping the hot curling iron on her client's shoulder. "Okay, okay, Ije calm down, calm down, I know . . . I know, just try and keep the kids safe. I'll call your brother right away."

The Yellow Cab dispatcher paged me on the emergency line the "go home" dictate. There was no passenger in my cab at this time (thank God), and no pickup in chase. I rushed home immediately.

Soaked and wet—the three perfect words to describe the ruins that I saw when I came home.

"Ije! Ije!" I called, my heart racing.

"We are up here, brother," she replied, "in my room."

I rushed upstairs to my sister's bedroom door.

"Daddy I soyyee, I soyyee, Daddy," cried our little bugger—I mean boy. He was wrapped in bedsheet, clinging to his auntie's arm, and so was his sister, all three atop the bed.

"That's okay, baby," said my wife, who came rushing past me, lifted him off the bed into her arms, and patted him on the back. "That's okay."

Relieved and grateful that my sister and the kids were all safe and dry (in her room, the only un-drenched part of the house, it seemed), I turned and tiptoed over to our bedroom.

With all the water drained out from the huge (rubber) mattress, our bed now looked like a mounted rectangular boat, with my wife's Holy Bible (the King James Version, which she always placed under her pillow) now at the center, soaking wet, like everything else. Yeah, everything on the floor was soaked, including her shoes—lots of them—and some of her un-hung bags.

I stood by the bed, shaking my head. "This boy. This boy, my own son, has truly brought this . . . this terrible hurricane to my house today."

"Hurricane?" my wife shouted from the hallway. "It's not my son that brought water into our bedroom in the first place. You did."

At this point in time, I couldn't tell which was more painful to bear, the soggy destruction before my eyes or the piercing dagger in her voice.

There was a brief silence, followed by what sounded like bangs of thunder in my ears.

"No-more-water-bed-in-this-house. Ever!"

And she has every right to be mad as hell. She does. After all, the waterbed thing was all my idea in the first place. My dream bed it was, now ruined, by own son.

I scratched my head, pondering, "Why is he always poking his hands and nose in wrong places, destroying everything? Why? Even when you think you've hidden every tool from his sight and reach, this boy still comes up with new surprises. Why? Why can't my son stay calm and harmless, just for one day? Look at this, this mess."

I took a very, very deep breath and blew out a loud puff. "I guess you're right," I conceded quietly, leaning on the right edge of the wooden box. "You are definitely right, baby sister. My daughter has never given me these kinds of headaches. Not even close, not for one day."

With my right hand, I reached down to the center of the bed and picked up my wife's Bible. It felt like a piece of dead wood washed off the shore, still a-dripping.

"Okay, no big deal," I said to myself, standing straight over the bed and pressing at the Bible hard with both hands. "I accept the consequences." Evidently another chapter in my "post-bachelorship" chronicle had revealed this wisdom: not every charm or romance of single life fits squarely into marriage. Especially when married with children.

In addition, I was noticing progressive similarities between my own mother and the woman who is now my wife. I swear.

"Babe, please pick up your clothes from the floor," my wife would grumblingly remind me, "and please, please don't be piling all these dishes in the sink for me.

I am not your mother." And believe you me, this was an everyday occurrence in our house.

"But you are beginning to sound like her," my mouth would like to say in reply, but my head always flashed an opposite reflex over my lips, forcing them inward, like a cork. My cheeks would bulge, though, a-grinning quietly, just like my father's would. Hmm. You know, now that I have time to think about it, I never ever saw nor heard my father utter more than three words every time there was an argument between him and Mother. He would just grin and reach for his leather-covered Holy Bible (the only one of its kind in the village then). The book of Solomon was his favorite of the holy book. And by the time he had done reading the first verse of the chapter of his choosing, a sort of quiet or peace beyond all understanding followed. Yeah, a very good Christian my father was, I grant you that, and a great husband and father to us too. We all miss him. Dearly.

I've digressed a little, pardon me.

It would be five days before we could get our new complete bedroom set delivered. And this time, my wife's choice: a higher elevated king-sized no-float mattress; Romanesque head and footboards with adjoining beautiful gold handle dressers on each side of this prominent headboard that looks like it's been carved out of a true mahogany. I must concede here that this new set, chosen by my wife, gave our bedroom the sort of solemn hue and flavor we never had before. She was very happy, and due to the simple fact that the whole set ended up costing me much less, I was happy too.

It's been eighteen years now, and we still have the same bed. Not a scratch yet on that Romanesque headboard, no fading, and not even a slight dip in the ever-sturdy mattress. And although once in a while I miss the soothing warm waves of my old bed, I've since adapted comfortably to our new mattress.

As for my wife, she continues to enjoy her exclusive "right" to the right side of the bed, which is also closer to the door (even though she never, never answers the doorbell). "Babe," she'll say, shaking me up every time there is a knock at the door, "see who is at the door."

And did I ever mention that the right side of this bed is also adjacent to the master bathroom door, meaning she never had to journey around the bed at night to use the bathroom, like I always do?

But I never complain about all that stuff. I always remember what an old friend of mine said at our wedding reception: "In order to maintain a peaceful and fantastic bedroom atmosphere, the man needs to complain about nothing." Well, he was right, to a certain degree.

You see, I try to go to bed before my wife does, and when I do, I tend to sleep like a baby. And never a night with nightmares. Dreams? Sometimes. Brief and always flying when I do dream. Arms spread wide and flapping like an eagle, my legs gliding like a curious diver. But I always find myself sky high, overlooking some colorful vegetation. My dreams never really made much sense to me, and I never cared either, for they are gone and vanished as soon as my eyes come open. If my wife ever falls asleep before I do, I always have to stretch the bed sheet up enough to at least cover my ear. I have to. For many years now, I have tried and applied everything I could place my hand on to stop her from snoring. Nothing has worked. I truly love my wife, and I know she feels the same for me, if not more, but it's that noise from her sleep that irritates the hairs in my ears. So I have to cover my ears, always.

Part of the problem really is her beloved sleeping position. Supine. And when (with a little divine help) I convince her to lie on her side, which helps to muffle the air a little, thirty minutes later my wife is on her back again and sounding like an idling old automobile with some valve problem. I'm not kidding.

Even after exhausting packets and packets of sleeping pills, silent nights are still a rarity in our bedroom. But she never believes me when I tell her she snores in her sleep. Oh no, my wife gets religious quick. Even as I tried to shake the annoying sound off her chest this early morning.

"God forgive you, for you know not what you do" was her instant response, her palms clasped above her chest, just like in a real prayer. "God, forgive, for you don't know—"

"What you mean I don't know what I'm doing? I'm trying to stop you from snoring."

"What's the matter with you," she fussed as I shook her left arm again. "Why don't you let me sleep?"

"Because your loud snore won't let me sleep either," I replied.

She grimaced a little. "I wasn't snoring. I was just having a good dream, and now I can't even remember what the dream was about."

"Thank God," I said. "Every time you dream, someone dies. Always about death."

"Liar." Now she is really awake. "You don't know anything about my dreams."

"I probably don't," I replied. "But they are not very good."

She sat up. "I do dream good dreams too," she said. "What about the night I dreamt about my mother coming back?"

"That's exactly my point babe. You always dream about the dead and gone."

She ignores my comment. "But three months later, my niece called me, telling me that she was pregnant with a girl."

"Yeah?

"And when the baby was born, it was obvious, my mother had come back. Even my brother knew that to be true."

"Are you saying your brother too—?"

"He did," she cut in, "and rightfully named his granddaughter Nne-Nna."

She then turned her head toward me and said, "Now what do you have to say about that, my doubting Thomas?". "That's just one dream in a million; the rest are nightmares. Do you know how many times you've woken me up in the middle of the night screaming in your so-called dreams?"

She blew out a loud puff and rolled her eyes up the ceiling.

"You know babe, I really think it's them late-night horror movies. And I will be glad when you learn to sleep on your side just, just like me."

"Leave me and my TV alone," she retorted. "And I am sick and tired of your early morning unsolicited lecturing. Stop it!"

I took the covers off, put my left arm over her chest, and said, "I am sorry babe, I was just trying to help."

She quickly took my hand off her chest. "I don't need this kind of help, not for my sleeping and definitely not for my dreams."

She stepped out of the bed and walked into the bathroom.

"Come on now babe. Even big dreamers need a little help and blessings too, from past great dreamers, I grant you that."

She gargled with the light-blue Listerine on the cabinet and spit.

"Big dreamers?" she queried. "Who do you really know that is a B-I-G dreamer? Name one person?"

"Easy, OBAMA!"

Now that really got her loose. She instantaneously let out a soft smile, rolling her head in a sort of partial agreement, and said, "But BARACK is his first name, you know, which means 'the blessed one' in Swahili" (she probably got that from a Kenyan friend of hers, I think). She shook her head, waving her right hand above her head, and said, "My dear, BARACK OBAMA don't need no help or blessing from no body."

"Oh yes he does. Correction, he did. Yes indeed."

"From who, God?"

"That too, and more."

"Huh?"

I cleared my throat and said, "OBAMA'S many blessings are of God. I do not dispute that. His big dream to be the President of the United States is innately linked to visions, predictions, and prophesies from a host of great dreamers. Yes, from the past."

She came back from the bathroom and sat down by the edge of the bed.

"Okay, tell me what I don't know. Who are these so-called great dreamers?"

I cleared my voice again and moved up close to the head of the bed.

Ever since this OBAMA phenomenon grabbed my attention, especially on the subject of "change," I began to do my own research, and I have been waiting for a day like this to reveal what I've found.

"You see babe," I began, "many, many years ago, years before the Dunhams' grandparents even migrated to America, a gentleman named Bartolomé de las Casas, a unique Spanish Colonist, came to the West Indies. He also knew Columbus—remember Christopher Columbus, the Spanish sailor who lost his way in the ocean and mistakenly landed in the shores of America?"

"Wait a minute," my wife said, "now w-ai-t a minute. Who is Dunham, and what does the Spanish guy—Bartolomé Casa or whatever you call him—have to do with BARACK and this presidential election?"

"Well, the Dunhams babe," I explained, "were BARACK OBAMA's mother's parents."

"Okay."

"And the Spanish guy—Bartolomé—was also a priest, a historian, and a humanitarian advocate."

"Advocate. Okay, go on."

"Yes, this priest—Bartolomé—upon his arrival to this new world they called America, put on his humanitarian vest, so to speak, stood up, and became a very strong advocate not only against the cruel maltreatments of the native 'Indians' at this time but also for blacks, who had been brought over by his fellow Spaniards as slaves."

"Now that priest," said my wife, "was really a godly man."

"He was indeed. All Bartolomé de las Casas wanted was freedom, fairness, and equality for all mankind."

"And you would think that human beings that call themselves Christians would understand such basic truth," my wife said.

"Unfortunately not babe. Not if greed and selfishness are at the head of their dreams. But thank God for people like Bartolomé de las Casas, who cared for their fellow beings. And for his relentless and unprecedented advocacy, he was dubbed as the Father of Liberation Theology, anti-imperialism, and anti-racism."

"But this priest, Bartolomé," she asked "he could not have dreamt or imagined way back then an Obama for president?"

"Maybe not, but his call and advocacy in humanitarianism, albeit hundreds of years ago, may have helped to prune mankind's conscience, to progress with change and accommodate such a righteous social parity as being witnessed today."

"Parity, you may have a point there," she said. "And who else was dreaming big, and how did you know all this anyway?"

I reached over to my desk, picking up the list that I had recently researched and compiled. "It's all in here, babe," I said. She took a quick look at the front page and nodded.

I then began to read the contents. She sat squarely and listened with the intensity of a good but curious student, interrupting only when necessary as I read my brief chronological profiles of some past great dreamers and advocates (and please, I apologize for any omissions—and there are probably many of them—in this advocacy chronicle; I am in no way a historian or a professor of history), whom by my computation may have foreran and foretold the coming of a President OBAMA.

Abraham Lincoln, I read on, the sixteenth president of the Union, was an outspoken opponent of the expansion of slavery in the United States. He introduced measures that resulted in the abolition of slavery, issuing the Emancipation Proclamation in 1863.

"President Lincoln, God bless his soul," she said. "Wasn't he from Chicago, Illinois, just like OBAMA?"

I let out a faint smile. Not because of her question but because of the way wife would always pronounce the "s" in Illinois. "Illinoi-s" she would say, just as she would stress the "s" in Des Moines.

"If they don't want you to say the letter S," she would argue, "they shouldn't have it in the word in the first place."

"Babe," I would try to explain, "that's because those names are probably French."

"French, my a . . . I am Igbo, honey, and in my language, you pronounce every word just like you see it."

"I know, babe" I said, kissing her slightly on her left chin. "And don't forget that I am Igbo too."

"But you like drinking French wine also," she retorted.

"French wines are delici-ous babe," I said, again, with the S silent.

"See, see how you end up sounding like a Frenchman, swallowing the S at the end of delicious too. Ridiculous."

I busted out laughing.

"You can laugh all you can," she said, her arms tightened across her chest, "but I know I'm telling the truth." She sighs.

"And you still did not answer my question about Lincoln," she reminded me.

"Of course. Lincoln was from Illinois all right, just like OBAMA. But from which city in Illinois, I'm not sure babe."

"And what makes you think that President Lincoln, over two hundred years ago, saw OBAMA coming?"

"President Lincoln may not have physically seen OBAMA," I replied, "but the vision of the Emancipation Proclamation may have set the stage for change. Change for equality, and Change for justice, for all. Just as the Founding Fathers meant it in the drafting of the American Constitution."

She folded her lips inward and nodded twice.

A few years later, I read on, it was W. E. B. Du Bois on the advocacy platform. And this time, a black man. He was one of the best scholars on social issues, a writer, and a great educator of his time. He was also the first black American to earn a Ph.D. from Harvard University.

"Harvard," my wife asked, "isn't it the same university OBAMA attended?"

"Exactly. And what a coincidence."

"This is getting interesting," she said, laying back down with both hands hugging tightly over her chest. "Please, babe, continue."

In Mr. Du Bois's relentless quest for equality and social justice for all," I read on, "he published a sociology research paper in early 1900s at the University of Pennsylvania titled 'The Philadelphia Negro,' and as a result he was rightly acknowledged as the Father of Social Science."

He therein wrote, "It revealed the Negro group as a symptom, not a cause; as a striving, palpitating group, and not an inert, sick body of crime; as a long historic development and not a transient occurrence."

On the returning black soldiers from WWI, who faced systemic mistreatment and racial discrimination, Du Bois also wrote in the Editorial page of *Crisis* magazine, which he founded,

"By the God of Heavens, we are cowards and jackasses if now that the war is over, we do not marshal every ounce of our brain and brawn to fight the forces of hell in our own land.
We return.
We return from fighting.
We return fighting.
Make way for Democracy!
We saved it in France, and by the great Jehovah, we will save it in the United States of America, or know the reason why."

"Yes brother Du Bois," my wife chimed in, pronouncing the S again here, "I would like to know the reason why myself."

"According to my little research," I went on, "Du Bois wrote relentlessly on social and political injustice of his time. He also dreamt about 'saving Democracy' in his land, the USA, way back in early 1900s."

"Boy, this guy sure was a hard-hitting activist, I say."

"He really was babe, but he was so frustrated with America shuffling her feet on parity, he even left the country and became a naturalized citizen of Ghana."

"Hh-hh-hh!" my wife shook her head. She clasped her palms as if in prayer and said, "Now, dear W. E. B. Du Bois, I hope in your Jehovah spirit, it should suffice to know that in this very year of our Lord two thousand and eight, your noble dreams for equality and social justice for all are finally coming to fruition. May your long tormented soul finally rest in peace, albeit oceans away from your beloved native land. Say Amen!

I did.

Dr. Ralph Bunche, the first person of color to receive the 1950 Nobel Peace Prize (for his successful mediation in Palestine), authored a pamphlet entitled "A World View of Race," in which he stated, "And so class will some day supplant race in world affairs. Race war will then be merely a side-show to the gigantic class war which be waged in the big tent we call the world."

"You mean Dr. Bunche had a dream about 'this day' too, just like Dr. Martin Luther King? Wow!"

"That's what I've been trying to tell you. This is no accident, babe. Just listen, I have more to come.

Then came the Medgar phenomenon.

Medgar Evers was born in 1925 in Decatur, Mississippi, a place where blatant discrimination was a cultural norm. He saw and experienced discrimination and racism even as early as first grade "with white kids in their school buses throwing things" at him and "yelling filthy things." Mississippi was a place where blacks dared not speak of civil rights much less actively campaign for them. Medger was a committed member of the NAACP and wanted to do everything he possibly could to change the psyche and culture of his native state.

Medgar Evers paid for his convictions with his own life, "becoming the first Major Civil Rights leader to be assassinated in the 1960s."

Myrlie Evers, his wife, said of her husband in *Esquire* magazine, "Medgar didn't want to be a martyr. But if he had to die to get us that far, he was willing to do it."

*Esquire*'s contributor Maryanne Vollers also wrote, "People who lived through those days will tell you that something shifted in their hearts after Medgar Evers died, something that put them beyond fear . . . At that point a new motto was born: After Medgar, no more fear."

Now, Medgar Evers probably didn't dream to take the black man this far, as is being witnessed today. Or did he?

"I'm starting to really believe it, babe," said my wife, nodding her head in a very slow motion. "It was all in the dream."

"Yes!"

"Wow, babe" she said, "you are really on to something. Please continue."

"Thanks, babe," I said, flipping to the next page of my notepad.

"Now, Rosa Parks. Remember the lady from Montgomery, Alabama, who on December 1, 1955, refused to give up her seat in the front section of the bus so a white man could seat. Who as a consequence was jailed for her civil disobedience?"

"Isn't that a bitch. I sure don't blame her."

"Neither do I. All this hard-working forty-two-year-old seamstress wanted was just a bus ride home after a long day's work."

"Poor girl," my wife said, "she must have been tired to her feet."

"Probably. But they still took her off the bus and dragged her to jail."

My wife's lips and eyelids tightened. "Cruel, insensitive bastards! Her mouth exploded, clenching her fists hard.

Now, Ms. Parks probably did not wake up that December morning and after brushing her teeth said to her mirror, "Mirror, mirror, on the wall, I am Rosa Parks, and I'm gonna change the world today." But her physical and mental tiredness, and the desire for simple human dignity, landed her in an Alabama jail, ironically exposing the endemic social cancer and bigotry in the American cultural fabric. As a consequence, a new era in the American quest for freedom and equality ignited.

While Ms. Rosa Parks lived to see white and black Americans sitting next to each other in Montgomery city buses and other buses and carriers all over the country, thanks to her civil disobedience, she probably never dreamt of all these other social changes. Let alone a black man sitting in the White House as a United States President. Lord, have mercy.

Or did she?

But Dr. Martin Luther King Jr. did.

He had "a dream, about this day."

As a young Baptist priest and social activist, I continued to read, Dr. King Jr. found himself thrust into the national spotlight in Birmingham due to all the raging social turbulence of these times. He helped organize a massive march to Washington D.C. on August 28, 1963. Several other religious leaders, labor leaders, and many black organizations were said to be amongst his partners. When they finally arrived at the Capitol, the marching crowd reportedly stretched from the Washington Monument to the Lincoln Memorial. Amongst the speakers at the rally were Charlton Heston, NAACP President-Roy Wilkins, and John Lewis—now US Representative for Georgia.

The floor having been warmed up by his speaking partners, Dr. King Jr. then delivered in his charismatic eloquence:

We cannot be satisfied as long as a Negro in Mississippi cannot vote, and a Negro in New York believes he has nothing to vote for. No, no, we are not satisfied, and will not be satisfied until justice rolls down like waters and righteousness like a mighty Spring . . . But I say to you today, my friends, so even though we face the difficulties of today and tomorrow, I still have a dream. It is a dream deeply rooted in the American dream. I have a dream that one day this Nation *will rise up and live out the true meaning of its creed: "We hold these truths to be self-evident: that all men are created equal," I have a dream today.*

I then put my notepad aside and turned to my wife and said, "Yes babe, I believe that Dr. Martin King Jr. truly had a dream about this day."

"More like a vision," my wife said. "I now believe Dr. King truly saw the vision."

I grinned heartily.

It is also very heartwarming to know that in this quest for simple human dignity, equality, and justice for all, many whites and many other non-black races, much more than are given credit, men and women of goodwill, have stood side by side, soul by soul, from the beginning of this long journey, to this day.

The Kennedys, for instance, starting from the late President John F. Kennedy, who, empathizing in the Black-American civil cause and acting contrary to the southern white Democratic anti-equality and anti-suffrage stance and psyche at the time, went ahead to endorse the Civil Rights agenda. He called for federal legislation to end racial discrimination in public accommodations and racial discrimination in employment.

Regrettably, President JFK was assassinated a few months later. But his death was not the end of the historic opportunity for racial change in America. In my opinion, it actually galvanized popular support for civil rights and other landmark social reforms.

His younger brother, Robert Kennedy, continued the fight for equality and social justice, just as his older late brother did. He even in his last public speech (before he too was assassinated), he predicted this day. RFK's amazing prediction I will explain later. And let's forever remember the landmark Civil Rights Act of 1964, signed into law by President Johnson. This finally outlawed discrimination (of blacks and other minorities) in schools, public places, and the workplace.

"But some white people I know," cut in my wife, "continued to discriminate."

I agreed. "But thank God still for a great many, many modern men of good will," I said, "men like Senator Ted Kennedy, for instance. In my opinion, Senator Kennedy is one of the few brave men alive who continue to work tirelessly for the true meaning of the Great American Creed and Dream."

"I like Ted Kennedy," said my wife. "With all the money in his family, he still fights for the poor."

I agreed.

"Then on January 28, Ted Kennedy himself took young Senator BARACK OBAMA in his own hand and, like a loving father, presented him to America and the world as the next President of America."

"I was deeply touched," said my wife, "when I saw the two of them on TV that day."

"Babe, in my opinion, that public display on national television had twin and prestigious symbolic meanings."

"Yeah?

"Well to me, it was like the passing of the torch, babe."

"Remarkable!" My wife shouted. "It's almost like the teen picture of Bill Clinton shown years ago, listening to then President Kennedy—awesome."

"Yes, babe," I said. "And there is something powerfully special when an elderly statesman stands by your side or behind you in a situation like this."

"Sure is."

"It reminded me of my uncle and I."

"Your uncle?" My wife asks. "Please tell me, babe, what happened?"

"Well, it was in my early teen years, barely two years after my dad's death," I began to recount, "I happened to get into a little trouble in the neighboring village, stupid little things little boys do all the time."

"Boys, of course," chimed in my wife. "But please go on, my ears are itching."

"Sorry, babe, I can't go into all the details now," I pleaded, "but anyway, the whole village, it seemed, some even with sticks and stuff, came marching into our compound."

"My goodness, babe, did you kill somebody or something? What did you do?" she insisted.

"Nothing like that," I replied. "But they told my uncle that while I was in their village, making some inquiries, I used a terrible language to describe an elder."

"What terrible language was that?"

"That I heard he acts with two hands in one arm."

"Oh my God, Babe." My wife laughed until tears dripped down her chin. "You called a village elder a thief? I can't believe you, babe."

"Well, that's how the guy that sent me described him to me," I said. "And at the time, I never knew that's what that phrase meant."

My wife, still laughing, asked, "So what did your uncle do?

"Nobody messes with my uncle, you know," I said. "He stood by me throughout and none dared to get close to me at all. At the end, their leader even came and shook hands with my uncle, before the crowd dispersed without incident."

My wife exhaled loudly. "That sounds like a proverb I heard from my father a long time ago. He said, 'When an elephant stands up behind an antelope, the preying lion wags its tail and backslides, saying, 'I was just joking.''

She then looked at me from the corner of her left eye and said, "I knew you were a very bad boy in your early years, not even mentioning your run-ins with the village girls also."

I shrugged my shoulders, a-grinning. "Just a little, babe," I said, "but I was also the village soccer captain and the youngest choirmaster ever in our church and parish."

My wife closed her eyes and was quiet for about a minute. "By the way, how did we go from BARACK OBAMA to talking about your crazy teen life?"

"I guess because life, with its intricacy, babe, is a universal phenomenon. And in my opinion, so is BARACK OBAMA."

She nodded her head slowly, then said, "And did you also hear what Congressman John Lewis said about OBAMA at the convention? The man from Georgia that spoke at your commencement?"

"Yes, babe, what a powerful speaker he is."

"And didn't you mention at your graduation that Mr. Lewis was also a very good friend of Dr. King?"

"He sure was, babe," I replied. "And as I mentioned that day, Mr. Lewis shared the platform with Dr. King Jr. forty-five years ago, when he delivered his prophetic 'I Have a Dream' speech at that famous Washington rally."

"Mr. Lewis is sure a living legend himself," said my wife.

"He is, babe. Just listen to how he profoundly connects OBAMA to Dr. King's Dream:

"Tonight, we have gathered here in this magnificent stadium in Denver because we still have a dream. With the nomination of Senator BARACK OBAMA tonight, the man who will lead the Democratic Party in its march toward the White House, we are making a down payment on the fulfillment of that dream."

"That was a very moving statement by Mr. Lewis, I say," my wife said. "You could even feel the angels dancing and singing in high heavens that convention night."

I agreed.

Yes. Yes. Oh yes. We here give thanks to God for this dreamland, America. America the beautiful. Huzzah!

America, the land, whose beauty is richly colored in white, black, brown, yellow, green, blue, red, and all nature's hues betwixt.

America, the land where in the founders' hearts and minds, 'All men are created equal.'

America, the land where freedom, liberty, and the pursuit of happiness are all God-given rights. Yes, America.

The land where the respect for and preservation of human rights and dignity reign supreme. Always.

Oh yes, America, the land where hopes and dreams are still alive.

America, the land where anyone, from any background, from any corner of the earth, following one's dreams, can come and can aspire to any height, the sky's the limit. Yes, America, the dreamer's world. Hail, America, the promised land.

"But, babe," my wife said, "you've mentioned and talked about everybody else in your so-called dream tree except for one person."

"Who? I cannot possibly mention every name connected to this thing you know. Absolutely impossible babe, babe. I must restrict my discussion to those who are saliently important."

"Is BARACK senior, OBAMA'S father, not saliently important then?"

"Heavens, yes," I replied. "BARACK senior sowed the ultimate seed, of course, and I was just about to get into that phase of my story, see."

I showed my wife the paragraph that follows in my rough ten-page chronology. Without bothering to look at my papers, my wife, with a skewed smile, folded her arms tighter around her chest and said, "The ultimate seed, huh? I wonder what he used to sow that seed. Hmmm. Okay, don't mind me, babe, I was just checking. Please go on."

"Thanks, babe, for checking," I said with a quick, complimentary grin. "But I can show you how BARACK senior sowed the ultimate seed, if you insist."

She tapped me on my stomach, "Don't be silly now," she said. "Please go on. I really want to hear the rest of your story."

And so I continued to read the rest of my script. She listened.

"Some forty-something years ago," I read, "a young black college aspirant from a remote village in Kenya, Africa, came to this promised land, America, to pursue his educational dream. On the school campus, this young black man found favor in the eyes of a young beautiful white woman from the heartland. They fell in love, united, and gave birth to a child. They named him BARACK."

"And that means 'blessed' in Swahili," my wife said.

"Yeah. Now, BARACK's birth and life may not have been prophesied in Biblical terms, but the eyes and minds of some great dreamers and what I call sociopolitical predictors from the past may have seen it coming."

"Yeah, Dr. Martin Luther King Jr. in his 'I Have a Dream' speech, for sure," my wife said. "Exactly, babe. And did you know that Robert F. Kennedy forty years ago, in 1968, accurately made the same prediction: 'I predict that forty years from now,' RFK proclaimed in his last public speech, 'that a Negro will be sitting in the White House, just like my brother did' (referring to late President John Kennedy)."

"You don't mean it," my wife said, turning her whole body almost entirely toward me. "That even the brother of President Kennedy predicted this thing forty years ago is mind-boggling, babe. OBAMA is definitely not an accident, I swear."

"And you said that this prediction was made in 1968?"
"Yes!"
"And this is 2008, exactly forty years later?"

"Yes, babe, yes."

My wife nodded her head gently and said, "Forty days and forty nights, and now forty years." She exhaled, adding, "God always delivers his people in forty counts. Babe, this BARACK OBAMA thing is definitely God's hands at work."

"Without a doubt in my mind, babe. And although his mother was not by any means a Virgin Mary (which is a topic beyond the scope of this article), nor did the Three Wise Men from the east see the star in the sky, BARACK was born, in my opinion, just like Jesus, in a very, very socially toxic time. A time of great racial inequality, servitude, hate, prejudice, and much human suffering."

My wife closed her eyes and just shook her head.

"In a racially polarized heavenly white world on one side and hellish Negro world on the other, was BARACK born, defying Jim Crow caste."

"Oh mercy," my wife said with a loud voice. "I'm even surprised they did not try to lynch his father. God must have been protecting them all the time."

"No doubt, babe. OBAMA, born in an era of overt prejudice, abject poverty, and state-condoned social injustice in America. A time when the oppressed and discriminated finally had it up to their neck and as a result began to engage in several open civil revolutionaries, challenging these long-held socially sanctified repressive establishments against fellow humanity."

"Oh mercy. What a tempestuous time BARACK was born into."

"A tempestuous time, indeed," I echoed, pleasantly surprised at her excellent choice of word.

"But thanks to the relentless struggles and efforts of those long lines of unyielding social advocates," I continued to read, "the historic Civil Rights Act (by the Thirteenth and Fourteenth Amendments) was finally established in 1964."

"I have seen the picture at least three times now, where President Johnson was signing the Civil Rights Law, with Dr. Martin Luther King and friends standing and watching with awesome pleasure."

"Yes, babe," I said, "it was a very historic moment in the American social revolution."

My wife nodded intensely. "And what a difference a president's pen can make."

"The ultimate pen it is, I grant you that."

"But babe, now let's be real. Do you think that BARACK OBAMA, a black man, could really, really be elected President of America?

"Oh yes, babe," I said "I definitely think so."

"But I'm really afraid, babe," my wife said, shaking her head slowly. "I want to believe. But something still scares me. I really don't think America is ready for a black President. I wish . . ."

I put my script down on the side table and with my right hand reached around her shoulder and said, "Babe, you know in the beginning, I had my doubts and was afraid too, just like you. But the more I watch this guy speak, and the more I see the rich and diverse colors of people surrounding this black man, I've come to my own conclusion. Black or not, BARACK OBAMA is the one."

She grabbed my right fingers with her left and said, "I pray that you're right babe, I do."

"You see, babe," I continued, "yeah, BARACK may not have been born preordained or garmented in royalty like a typical king or from the bloodlines of past presidents, but when you watch him speak, just listen to what he says and how he says it. He is the one, babe. This young black man, bustling with unprecedented charisma, wit, and wisdom, he is the very one. And watch his style also. In my opinion, BARACK is the only one that's running the classiest campaign ever, a campaign of the twenty-first century indeed. Yes, he is the one. And did you not see how in Berlin the whole world stood up cheering and chanting, "Run, BARACK, run. Hail to OBAMA, hail. Now is the time, long live BARACK OBAMA."

"Imagine all the millions of people who came just to see and hear OBAMA," my wife said. "It was like Christ delivering His Sermon on the Mount."

"Except that unlike Jesus," I said, "BARACK is not here to sermonize for, redeem, or salvage lost souls. Never been his purpose. All those spiritual matters have already been settled on the cross by Christ himself, long, long ago."

"Hallelujah! Jesus is my savior, Hallelujah."

"But as for BARACK OBAMA, he is simply our flesh and blood, living in our times, the present, and feeling the pulse and pains of his fellow citizens. Yes he is. And with them big ears of his, BARACK is always listening, listening and reading the signs—"

"Signs," my wife cut in, "what signs?"

"The signs of the times, babe, these physical times."

There was a brief silence.

"But, you have to admit that there is still great danger out there," my wife worried, "especially with the clans people looking at a potential black president?"

"Of course. There's always some dangers in fighting for change. To some people, the word could be upsetting, as it is offsetting to their power grip. Just as the political and social establishment of Jesus's era—the strict conservatives of the time did not want to recognize him, let alone believe in his humane message—today the same extreme, like-minded conservatives, men so Adamic in their skullcap, are also, for lack of a better word, too obtuse to the signs of the times we live in."

My wife tapped me on my left thigh. "Babe, I hate it when you use those big words—obtuse, adamic. Please reserve those for your newspaper articles and stuff, not for me. I am your wife."

I turned and gave her a kiss on her chin. "I'm sorry, babe. I got carried away."

"I know."

"But what I'm saying is there are of course some folks out there who are adamantly opposed to, and even scoff at, OBAMA's views for the future of our nation as mere childish dream."

"It's really a shame that some people's hearts out there can be so hardened, so rock hardened, that an honest call for change gives them heartburn. It baffles me."

"Babe, that's the sad reality of our world, old as Adam, I grant you that."

"But this is the twenty-first century. People should wake up."

"Well said, babe. Some will, some won't. Those who have woken indeed understand the progressive value in change and are now streaming to the OBAMA camp— black, white, brown, yellow, red, and all the in-betweens— evidencing a social-physical melting phenomenon of the changing times."

"Isn't that the truth."

"For in him and with him," I said, "all human racial boundaries converge, melt, and become one."

"And what a new world order such would be. Just Imagine!" my wife exclaimed, as she got up from the bed again and headed for her morning showers.

Now, imagine for one minute, America in her early 1960s, this young boy of biracial parents, a white mother from the heartland and father from the black Afrikan nation of Kenya. And his name, BARACK. A name so foreign it was funny to the native ear. He probably grew up too experiencing the same development path of most youths his age. Kind and time, he struggled to understand life, with all its perplexities, the ever-changing neighborhoods, bundled with prejudice, rejection, street fighting, love, and hate. He probably cried for help every now and then and got in a jam, frustrated at things happening to him he couldn't understand. As a young teen, seeking some form of identity, BARACK probably experimented with a few novelties, some rational, some irrational, like smoking a joint or even chasing rats and grasshoppers in his neighborhood yards and fields. Some wild sport, I grant you that.

Later, as a young adult, while on a roots expedition to his father's land, BARACK even slept on floor mats many nights, in a mud house, with his African relatives, in Kenya. From the same warm brownish clay pot, with bare fingers, BARACK probably savored *ugali*, yes *ugali*, day after day, with all his half brothers and sisters—the OBAMA clan. A-ha.

It must be noted here too that it was really the American side of his family, the Dunhams, mother and grandparents, who not only raised him but did their utmost to protect and shield young BARACK from most of the aforementioned social thorns and blades of the times. Most Christians, including myself, that treasure the inherent lessons and wisdom in the Bible, find several verses replete with "divine protection of His chosen vessels," until their mission on earth has been accomplished. Baby Jesus, for instance, was hustled away from Israel into Egypt by his parents to escape the "jealous blade of King Herod." But why Egypt? I ponder, at times. Yeah, why and how could baby Jesus and his foreign-looking parents have lived, undetected, amongst the native peoples of Egypt? Huh?

Pardon me, I digress again, but that's a curious and interesting topic for another time. Back to BARACK. Now.

Having been raised with a good upbringing, it is my belief that BARACK knows and feels the pulse, pains, and sufferings of most Joes and Marys in his world. Yes, the normal everyday humans who are struggling day in and day out to make ends meet, especially in these times.

BARACK, like a host of other concerned and insightful minds out there, feels that in the last seven and half years, the leadership of his beloved country of America has been steering America the great onto an alarmingly disastrous path, the Bush path, consequently creating bleeding, heartache, and suffering for millions of his fellow citizens. He sees and reads every day of hundreds of businesses closing (many due to outsourcing), creating massive job loss and trickle-down hardships. People who used to eat on the table are now scraping their tiny remaining leftovers from the floor of the kitchen and wondering what will happen tomorrow.

His heart breaks when he sees or hears of our young men and women being shipped into harm's way, some on their third or fourth trips, with no guarantee of coming back alive to their loved ones. His heart breaks when he sees or hears of very hardworking folks losing their dream homes in droves, with more people now than ever sinking into the poverty well. And the sick? They too now have become social sinners. They can't be saved or get treated because they either do not possess health insurance or to have been rejected for the reason of "pre-existing conditions." Huh?

"America, how many more years can your people sit and endure hard times? OBAMA wondered. "And how did this great land of dreams turn into the most unintelligible bed of nightmares?"

Still, her people wake up every morning agape. Regular, hardworking folks wake up wondering if they can even afford to buy food or send their children to school anymore.

Complicating this all, America is enmeshed in a not-so-popular war at this point in time without end in sight, and the rest of the world is gaping at us, wondering, "What's wrong with America?"

"There is nothing wrong with America," OBAMA seems to proclaim to fellow citizens and to the rest of the world. I paraphrase: "The wrong is with her leadership, not with her people, no, not with the good, hardworking people of America."

Thirty minutes later, my wife finally came out of the bathroom smelling like a blend of rose and peach, hair raised up in a ponytail, and her lips adorned in glossy deep red. Fresh.

"Oh, babe," I said, straightening up in bed and rubbing my hands together, smiling, "you smell so delicious this morning. Why don't you come over here so I can check you out."

She flagged her left hand, reached into her dresser, and pulled out some undergarments. "Sorry, loverboy," she said as she slipped into something dark red, "you missed your chance last night."

"It's the foofu, babe," I replied. "You know I can't keep my eyes open thirty minutes after that good stuff."

"Well, babe, in this case, that good stuff has taken the place of this good stuff, for now. And shouldn't you be getting ready for work yourself?"


### Who Can I Send? Here I Am, Send Me
*December 2006*

As he vacationed with his wife and children in Hawaii, far away from politics and the press, BARACK OBAMA continued to ponder and ponder at the plight of the nation he loves, the ever-bleeding hearts of families in harm's way, the ever-shrinking job market, unending home foreclosures due to a sinking economy, with more and more children with their parents forced to sleep in bags, or if lucky in makeshift shelters. He is sickened, sickened that 30 to 40 percent of American children, children of the richest nation on earth, cannot afford to be sick, because parents have no access to healthcare.

It was probably there and then that he seemed to have received the ultimate call, almost like in the scriptures: "Who can I send, and who will go for us?"

But before he said a resounding "Yes Lord, send me," OBAMA probably asked himself two big questions: (a) "Can my family survive the rigors of a presidential campaign? My wife being an extraordinary woman and my children above average, I conclude they can manage it," he reasoned. (b) "Is there something I can provide more effectively than all these other candidates? Yes, I can bring the country together, break up some old, sterile arguments, make sure we are speaking honestly with American people, and bring them into the process of change," so he concluded.

On February 11, 2007, at the steps of Illinois State House, BARACK OBAMA declared his candidacy for the presidency of the United States of America. Change is now on board.

Change. But can America truly, and I mean *truly*, go for it? Can America retire the old and bankrupt and hire the feisty, young, and vivacious? Is it time, finally?

Carried by the animated wind of hope from all corners of America, OBAMA'S tide and call for change began to spread like wildfire, headed straight toward Washington.

### Change? Yes We Can

On May 3, 2007, on *Larry King Live*, when Ms. Oprah Winfrey, who had never openly supported a political candidate before, threw her unequivocal support/approval for OBAMA, did she see something in her crystal ball that changed her mind?

I wonder.

When a legitimate son of a white American mother and a black African father, once a Jim Crow taboo, is now a central American politico-attraction and just a few steps away from the White House, is it in the spirit of the changing times?

On October 1, 2007, Tyra Banks presented him with a crystal ball and asked, "Senator, what do you see?"

"I see the White House" was his quick answer. Simple but brave.

Wow! The White House in a crystal ball?

Not as a spectator? Not as a yardman or housekeeper? Not even as the venerable presidential doorman?

None of these. BARACK OBAMA, a black man, had just seen the White House from a presidential crystalline lens.

Brilliant. But as a black aspirant to that *White's House*, OBAMA would face torrents of threats and insults and have to work ten times as hard as his white candidates. Can BARACK OBAMA do all that?

In my opinion, yes he can.

One mid-summer Monday afternoon, as I was about to leave my office for my lunch break, John, the publisher of a local newspaper that I send articles to once in a while, met me at the door.

"Good morning, Big John," I said, stretching out my right hand to him. I personally prefixed "big" to his name the first time we met, because standing at about six feet two, with a barrel chest, and weighing over 240 pounds, John has the posture and gait of a giant when he walks.

He glanced at his wristwatch before grabbing my hand. "Doc, it's 1:30 p.m., not morning."

"In my world, Big John, everything in life always begins in the morning, clock or no clock. And you better get that in your head."

Big John laughed exuberantly. "You sure know how to get somebody's eyes blinking, Doc," he replied, as we did our hand-and-fist thing.

"I really stopped by to see if you have anything for our next month's publication, especially with the election heating up, and OBAMA, a potential black president? Man, I bet you got something to say about that."

I don't usually write on politics, but this OBAMA movement is exceptionally special, I thought.

"Let's do lunch if you have time," I said, pushing on the glass door handle and leading the way out. "I have a lot to say about that guy."

The restaurant is only a few minutes' walk across the street from my office and is sparsely populated this Monday afternoon.

"How can I help you?" the manager asked as we walked in. He is either Korean or Taiwanese, but I've never bothered to ask. I told him it was not takeout, that we were sitting for our lunch. He took the orders from the front desk.

I ordered chicken-fried rice, and Big John beef with fried rice. Since it's one of those places you don't have to wait to be seated, we took an empty table (for two) in the southeast corner. The manager came back a minute later with two glasses of cold water. I requested, in addition, hot green tea.

"Would you like sugar or honey for your tea, sir?"

"No, thank you," I replied, "just the tea."

"And can I have a large Coke with lots of ice, please?"

"Sure!" the manger replied. "One green tea, one large Coke with ice. I bring for you."

"But Doc, how can you drink hot tea in this 85-degree heat?" Big John asks as he pulls a long notepad out of his briefcase.

"Did you not order for a large Coke?" I asked humorously.

"Of course I did. What's your point, Doc?"

"That cup of ice-cold Coke, Big John, has more fire in it than my hot tea, I grant you that."

"Now that's the craziest thing I've ever heard."

"Crazy but true. You see, Big John, that cup of soda you just ordered is loaded with grams and grams of sugar and caffeine, not to mention chemical preservatives not necessarily kosher for life. So what do you think all that stuff does to your body?"

"Keep me cool," Big John replied.

"No, brother," I said, "they set all your organs, your internal being, on fire."

Big John's countenance changed. "Man, I have been drinking pop since I was a kid," he said. "I haven't melted yet. Doc, quit playing with my head."

"I am certainly not playing, Big John," I said. "That you can't see what I'm saying now does not mean it's not happening. Our body is, by nature, very patient, highly tolerant, and handsomely forgiving."

"I'll drink to that."

"Sugar, in my opinion, is only sweet at the tongue. Past the tongue, and especially loaded in the bloodstream, sugar can be a bitter evil your creator warned you about, but that's a great topic for another time. Now, coupled with all that caffeine, sugar gives your body a box-load of energy, which is good if you are out there digging up soil, like farmers used to do. Or if you are like the Williams sisters, hopping around on a tennis court all day long. Or like Kobe and all the other high-energy-venting athletes out there playing on either basketball courts, football fields, or racetracks. Then, you have my wholesome permission to sugar load."

"So, because I am neither an athlete nor a country farmer, I cannot enjoy my ice-cold pop, even on this hot, sunny afternoon? You are definitely an appetite downer, Doc, I grant you that."

The manager came back with our beverages.

As I opened my teabag's wrapping and inserted the bag into the small cup of hot water, I noticed Big

John hesitating to put his fingers around his large cup placed in front of him. With strange eyes, he looked at the large plastic cup, still holding fast to his half-full glass of drinking water.

"Sorry, Big John," I said, pointing to his notepad, "Pardon me, I kind of went off on a tangent. You wanted to know my opinion about OBAMA, right?"

He cleared his voice, pulled out his pen from his shirt pocket, and said, "Yes, Doc. In your opinion, who is BARACK OBAMA? Why should a common American like me vote for him?

"A very good and legitimate question indeed," I said. "It is the trillion-dollar question that must be rightfully addressed, because it's about time we the people understood the true meaning and awesomeness of the American presidency. It is about time we realize that the extraordinary times and circumstances we find ourselves today definitely demand an extraordinary leadership."

"So, do you think BARACK OBAMA is the right choice then?" Big John asked.

"Well, according to his opponents, BARACK OBAMA is *that one. That one* who wants to be president. *That one* who has not yet been tested. Tested with a big T."

"Now, you lost me already," Big John said raising his pen up. "What do you mean by tested?"

"Meaning BARACK has not been schooled in the Virtual Washingtonian College of Presidency, has no long political testimonials, and perhaps no physical scars on his forehead or on his nose seen by the human eyes. So, his opponents claim BARACK OBAMA has not been tested."

"Tested and schooled for the American presidency? By whom?" Big John asks. "Is not the American populace the true testing body of a presidential candidate?"

"Absolutely. And that's what the campaign and election November 4 is all about," I said. "The day American citizens truly exercise their ultimate right, the right to dish out a 'P' for President or an 'F' for follower."

"P or F," echoed Big John with a big grin, "and no in between. I like that, Doc."

"And the loser can't event apply for VP either."

"Hell no," Big John said. And after taking his first gulp of his Coke he said, "That's not the American way, Doc."

I agreed.

"But going back to the so-called untested claim by OBAMA'S opponents," Big John again pried, "what criteria would you surmise such is based on?"

At this point, the waiter came back with our lunch orders and placed them perfectly on the table.

"Enjoy your meal" he said, then disappeared to the kitchen area.

I took a full scoop of my rice. It was hot and spicy, just the way I like it. I then took a sip of my water and said, "Okay," responding to Big John question. "Okay, just relying on bare hunch here, Big John, I assume the following:

a.  Since BARACK has never served or partaken in a legally or traditionally declared/approved war, like in Vietnam, or recently Iraq, he, BARACK, has never been tested.
b.  Since he's not "old enough," or since he has not served in the Senate for at least three terms, partaking and chairing specific committees, he, BARACK, has never been tested.
c.  Since he's never been a mayor of any American city or governed any large State in the union for one day, like Alaska, where there are probably

more wild lives than humans to govern, and therefore, frequent animal casualties, a sort of unique sport, for even the governor . . ."

I scooped another mouthful of my rice and chewed without haste as I watched Big John do the same with his right hand but at a much faster pace. He wrote with his left. "Therefore," I continued after swallowing, "a simple political rookie like BARACK OBAMA, in their muddled judgment, has never been tested."

Big John stopped writing and leaned back on his chair, letting out a loud puff of air.

"Well, Senator McCain and his darling quality-control testers," he said, "I pray thee all to try growing up black, in a good-old white America. Imagine for one second in your privileged life growing up as a child, a living offspring of a once derided and tabooed human relationship, a white woman, bearing a child for a black man."

"Hello, John Crow! I chimed in."

"But back to the real questions that Americans are asking: "Who is BARACK OBAMA? *What* makes BARACK tick? What inspires BARACK? How did BARACK come so far so fast?"

"Again those are critical questions Big John," I said. "You see, brother, with so little and such sparse testimonials in his thin portfolio, it might seem unimaginable that young inexperienced OBAMA can qualify and rise to the seat and responsibilities of American presidency, right?"

"Right."

"But, my friend, note this down. Qualifications we acquire, but virtue we are born with. BARACK OBAMA is a virtuous man. He is so real and yet so simple. Just listen to or read an excerpt from his party's acceptance speech in the packed Denver Broncos Stadium in August 2008, and I quote, "I realize that I am not the likeliest Candidate for this Office. I don't fit the typical pedigree, and I haven't spent my career in the Halls of Washington. But I stand before you tonight because all over America, something is stirring. What the nay-sayers don't understand is that this Election is never about me. It's about you, you, you."

"What a virtuous man indeed BARACK OBAMA is."

"Atop all virtues evident in BARACK is the president who would be the leader of the twenty-first century. The leader that can bring the rest of the nations together in one accord, conveying the simple reality: we are all members of a human race, belonging to the same planet, breathing the same air, and feeding from the same soil."

"Good Lord, Doc," Big John said, "you are truly passionate about OBAMA. It's like you know him as family. You are convinced beyond any doubt now that BARACK OBAMA is the one. The one chosen to move America forward."

"Listen, brother," I went on, "OBAMA is young, calm, and wise, with the jurisprudence akin only to King Solomon (without the many wives and concubines)."

"Not too fast, Doc," Big John said, putting his fork down on the napkin next to his nearly-emptied plate. "Don't count him out yet in that way, for in my opinion, men of big dreams have big appetites also. And besides, his father was African, who easily handled ten wives with no sweat."

I almost choked on my food laughing. "What tabloid have you been reading, Big John. OBAMA Senior never had that many wives, not even close."

"Ten wives or not," replied Big John, "that boy has big dreams, I swear."

"Of course he does. Who in his right mind would be running for president of the United States of America, unless he is of above normal intelligence and has big dreams."

"What about his wife?" Big John asked.

"Oh, Michelle, wonderful woman, I think."

"I like her, Doc. That woman's got assets." Big John drops his pen on the pad, raises both hands forward and drawing a virtual bi-convex to demonstrate his point. "I mean real good assets."

"Well, she is smart, tall, and beautiful. And from the looks of her hips, her gait, and her mannerisms, Michelle not only exudes the solid elegance of her ancestral African queenliness, but she also makes evident a very popular Igbo (Nigerian) idiom: '*Di-bu-nma-nwa-anyi.*' Translated in English: 'The true beauty of a woman is made evident in a good husband."

Big John quickly grabbed his pen. "Doc, please could you repeat that. I definitely want my wife to hear that."

"Wife number . . . what are we talking about?"

"Doc, how did you know? I never told you I was married before?"

"It's the African thing, brother, no sweat."

Big John shook his head, grinning. "Doc," he said, "you are too much. You should be running for the governor yourself, you are so cool, so smart, and so impressively insightful."

"Me, run for governor? Do you know what it costs just to run for local council? No, brother, I am not a politician. Like my father once said, politics is for lawyers and politicians. I'm neither. I am in the business of healing,

Big John. I wouldn't necessary claim that it's my call in life. But so far, I am enjoying my life."

The waiter came by to check on us. He reached down and picked up Big John's emptied plate and placed it on his tray.

"Yes, you can take my plate too," I said, placing my fork down next to my plate.

Big John took a strange look at my plate and said, "But, Doc, you only had half of your food."

"I am good, Big John," I said grabbing my teacup and took a sip of my green tea. It was cold.

"Can I have more hot water please?" I asked, holding the cup outward to him.

"Sure," the waiter replied, taking the cup off my hand. Turning to Big John he said, "And do you want another Coke, sir?"

Big John shook his head, waving his hand. "No more Coke for me," he replied, pushing the empty cup aside.

"My diet is usually half food and half fluid," I told Big John after our waiter left. "Hot tea mostly. And besides, I never finish all my dish—breakfast, lunch, or dinner, never."

"How come? You have some dogs in your house or something?"

"As a matter of fact, I did. Bingo was his name. The pet shop where we got it told us he was a hybrid of collie and husky. But in that dog's mind, he was my third child and would rather eat our leftover dish than dog food."

"Some lucky dog," said Big John.

"But my father never had a dog. He had only eleven of us and would always leave a bite or so for any one of us children that had the honor to pick up and clean up Papa's dinner plate."

"Eleven children! How many wives did your father have, Doc?"

"Wives? Are you kidding? My father was one of the most devout Christians I ever knew," I said. "Unlike his fathers, my father believed in one wife, and multiply."

"Eleven children from one woman," Big John said in a low, slick voice. "That's a lot of juicing and seeding, I grant you that. Don't they teach contraception in your country?"

"Brother, old-time Christian religion does not have a page in their Bible for prevention. Such a taboo could not even be discussed."

The waiter came back with a cup of hot water and another bag of the green tea. He placed those in front of me, including the check. I picked up the check, glanced at it, and handed it back to him with a twenty-dollar bill. "Keep the change," I said.

"Thank you, sir," he said, bowing. He left with a big smile on his face.

Big John took a quick look at the three pages he'd taken. He then asked, "So, Doc, how would you compare BARACK OBAMA to his opponents. How is he different?"

"Good question," I said. "OBAMA, unlike his challenger from the other side of the aisle, is young, charismatic, enthusiastic, insightful, energetic, and a breath of fresh air wherever he goes."

"I vote yes on that one," concurred Big John as he wrote.

"And unlike his opponent, BARACK OBAMA's campaign does not need to be pollinated, pulsated, or resuscitated. Never. He is BARACK, the 'blessed one.' And in my opinion, the only one still standing with life in abundance."

"BARACK, the blessed one, full of life. Yes, go on."

"BARACK OBAMA is a highly, I mean highly, educated young man. He is very witty and with a natural gift of oratory, reflecting a well-educated native speaker."

And the meteoric rise in popularity of this young African American man has not only mesmerized the nation and the world, but it has moved us as a nation into a new and higher social horizon and with a new national psyche and slang: *change*."

"Yes, Doc. Change—that seems to be the new sign of the times."

"Yes, brother. Change that will bring peace, with inherent prosperity. Peace—and not war and recession/ depression, evidenced in a misguided and inept administration, like we've had for seven years now."

"Yes, Doc, sail on."

"OBAMA believes that hard work should be rewarded handsomely, not punished with massive layoffs, job loss, home loss, and corporate greed!"

OBAMA believes that it is the leadership's inherent role to create an environment for economic and employment opportunities, both here at home and abroad, not make excuses for an unprecedented constellation of economic woes and long lines of unemployment.

Yes, OBAMA believes that opportunity, yes opportunity, should be made a building platform for all, not a monopoly for the privileged few.

OBAMA believes that a meaningful, comprehensive approach to educating the children of America is the best human investment for the future, not only for our country but also for the entire world we live in.

Yes, OBAMA believes that healthcare for every citizen should be a right. And rightfully so. Where is the heart and soul of the so-called Christian Nation if we can't take care of each other? Since when did Christianity become a 'password to life' instead of a 'lifestyle'? Shouldn't 'being your neighbor's keeper also include at least wishing your neighbor good health?"

"But Doc," Big John asks, "isn't there a better word to describe that: socialism?"

"Well, some cynics complain and shout 'socialism.' But the last time I checked, humans are still social beings, still living, breathing, and unconsciously communicating with one another everyday socially, albeit without the overt badge or stigma of the 'ism.' What is interesting too is that in a state of natural disaster or national crisis, like in a war or drastic economic crisis like we are facing today, everybody is asked to give up some individual liberties and anchor their ship, so to speak, to the central control, with the president, the decider."

"Yes, the president is the commander-in-chief all right," Big John said, "but we still have Congress to stop him."

"Well, Congress might still try to flex their muscles, maintaining a quasi check and balance table, but in general, the commander-in-chief gets his way with Congress to do as he chooses. And as the president continues to run the country, stressing individual sacrifice and working together, you find a lot of citizens with proclamations and badges saying, "Country first." Patriotism, some call it. And that's good and dandy."

"So what's wrong with country first?" Big John asks. "Sounds patriotic in my opinion."

"Not necessarily true, brother," I replied. "It's what gets lost or drowned in the psyche of overt patriotism that should concern every decent citizen."

"Like what?

"What concerns me, Big John, is the unconscious omission of the human element—the social web and glue, the true motto of the family of peoples that make up our country which is found in 'We the People,' rightfully and insightfully proclaimed by the founding fathers. We the People have now been deceitfully displaced by this abstract emblem: 'Country first,' and that's dangerous."

"Great point, Doc," said Big John. "I never saw it like that."

"It is my humble opinion," I continued on this point, "and for sure OBAMA'S also, that if all citizens of America would come together in a peaceful and amiable social bonding and replace the hypocritical 'country first' badge with a more meaningful and native 'We the People' invocation, the human race would forever be connected to each other. There would be mutual respect and care for each other. And it is under such native platform that a bill like a comprehensive healthcare plan for every member of the human family would be realized as a moral obligation and therefore welcomed with open hearts and minds. America will then be a celebrated healthier nation."

"And that's what a Christian nation should be," Big John added.

"Should, would, could. But are we? Truly?"

"Sometimes I wonder myself," replied Big John. "We say it, but we don't act it."

"Doesn't such have a name in the Bible?"

"Hypocrites!"

"Thank you brother," I said. "But let's move on to the future, the change that's come."

"I'm with you, Doc. Go on."

"It's my belief that BARACK OBAMA is dedicated to making America the leader once again in research and technological development. He believes that with genuine attention paid to research in every aspect of our industrial society, America can again regain her leadership in the industrialization of the twenty-first century, be it in education, sciences, arts, automobiles, energy, or health."

"Imagine how many jobs would be created," said Big John, "and how much happier people would feel again."

"That's what I'm trying to tell you. Peace, prosperity, and happiness are the blessed triplets of an OBAMA dream regime."

"Who can say nay to that?"

"It is the change, my brother, we need."

"Yes. And we can," Big John said.

"I read in his book, *The Audacity of Hope,* that young BARACK OBAMA, right out of law school, from one of the best schools in the nation, chose instead to take a job helping less fortunate people and victims fallen on hard times regain confidence in themselves and get back on their feet."

"Yes, he did."

"And while in Senate, albeit fresh on the seat compared to his aged peers, the young Senator from Illinois foresaw the grim difficulties, foolishness, and inherent misery in going to war, especially with a country that in no shape or form had attacked the United States on 9/11. Now, while most members of the Senate, including his Republican challenger to the White House, gave Mr. Bush the green light to go to war, BARACK OBAMA categorically voted no to the President's reckless war option. We now know the rest of the story, written in bloody disaster, which all brings us back to the most profound question: 'Who can you trust when it comes time to make a life-or-death judgment, putting American lives in harm's way?'

"Is it the wise and insightful one that gets it right from the beginning? Or would you rather trust your life and your loved ones to the hasty and hawkish arms of Washington politicians, who rushed to help Mr. Bush and his hawkish advisers send thousands of young men and women into harm's way, with grave consequences?"

"Not by my vote," said Big John.

"Are you still with me, brother?"

"Every inch of the way, Doc."

"And still a Christian?

"Doc, I read my Bible every morning, believe me."

"Good. In our Christian Bible, did not our Christ in his rebuke of Simon Peter's sword attack (before He was betrayed by Judas) warn His followers, and the rest of the human race, against such beastly acts?"

"'Those that live by the sword shall die by the sword' was his proclamation," said Big John.

"And so I ask this again and again, "When will Christians really put their egos aside and stop deceiving themselves and truly listen to and follow our savior's humane lifestyle—examples of peace, love, and hope? When?"

Big John stopped writing. He leaned back flicking his pen and said, "You know, Doc, I can see a parallel here."

"Yes, indeed."

"Something tells me that maybe, just maybe, in this young man called BARACK OBAMA, our savior's message of peace and love—for family, for our neighbors, for the country, and for the entire world—may soon be a living reality, just like Christ evangelized."

"That's the essence of OBAMA'S presidency, my brother," I said, involuntarily hitting the tabletop with my right fist. "A president that will embrace and advocate for peace and love. A president that can empathize with normal everyday people to help stop their bleeding and heartache. A president that would restore sanity and parity in their rightful civil seat, displacing the present psyche of insanity."

"But can one man do all these?" Big John asked. "Can OBAMA single-handedly wheel us out of this, this mess?

"I didn't say he'll do all these alone. However, with a good choice of competent wise men and wise women in his cabinet, BARACK OBAMA will reign high and forward with good will, restoring peace, hope, and joy to the world."

"I say amen to that, Doc."

"And I truly, truly have absolute faith and confidence in this man. I do."

"Doc, you sound like his press secretary already," Big John joked.

I smiled. "But if you could print this in your newspaper, so that many can read and understand," I said in reply, "each one of us has done our part presenting and promoting his cause."

"Well said, Doc. Please go on."

"Even in this present state of economic debacle, BARACK OBAMA stands his ground, calm and focused. While his opponents crisscrossed the country, tap-dancing around the economic fallout and making erratic outbursts, BARACK OBAMA got busy, assembling his group of shrewd advisers, deliberating, and looked for practical solutions, economic solutions that would focus on helping the Main Street of America, not feeding the greedy cats on the Wall Street. That's OBAMA."

"Yes, I was really impressed with his coolheaded demeanor," said Big John.

"You saw the true leader that he is, standing with his fellow distressed citizens and, feeling their pains, assuring America and the world that Americans are a resilient people. Reminding Americans that it is the challenges in the past that helped to make Americans a stronger and better people. And that by working together, 'these too shall come to pass' with victory."

Big John leaned back one more time. He put his forefinger in the air and said, "This, dude, will make a great president, I swear."

"You better believe it, brother," I said. "OBAMA listens to the people. He knows the people, he understands the people. OBAMA knows the issues at stake, and he understands that with change, real change, we can overcome in ways beyond expectations."

"And most real change," Big John said, "if it is to affect and benefit the future, begins with the young, not at old age anyway."

"Thank you, brother, and that's my point. Listen, I personally have nothing against old folks, believe me. After all, I just had my sixtieth, you know."

"Congratulation, Doc," said Big John. "You sure don't look a day past forty-five."

"Thank you very kindly. I overheard some folks in McCain's recent rallies, folks even older than him, squeaking and croaking, 'Change, change,' from the background, in between his speeches. I had to hold myself from laughing, you know. I then asked myself,

'Did I really hear the word "change" from those wrinkled old faces? And like OBAMA would ask, 'Change to what?'"

"But, Doc, this is a free country, and everybody, old or young, has the right to free speech."

"Of course they do," I said. "Tell me this. What types of change can we really expect at old age besides the normal wear and tear of aging body parts and wrinkles?"

Big John laughed till his pen dropped off his fingers. "You are the funniest guy I've ever met, Doc."

"Let us be real now. It is time for the old to step aside, honorably, and let the young come on board. Because any claim of vigor or valor past age sixty-five, no matter how much we dream, is usually in the past tense. Hello?"

"You definitely have a point there, Doc," Big John said, picking up his pen from the floor. "OBAMA is of the present, brother, and that's what I'm talking about. He is not only full of vigor. This vibrant phenomenon called OBAMA is nothing that America has ever seen before. And that, in my opinion, is not an accident."

"OBAMA phenomenon," Big John echoed, "not an accident. But why? I mean, what proof do you have to average readers that it's not . . . ?"

"An accident?" I said, "Not, with a big N. If you listen and watch him closely, you will see what I see, brother."

"And what do you see?

"An uncommon young man almost of divine calling, as they say in the biblical times, oh yes. Leaders like David, John the Baptist, Jesus, and even Mohamed. And also in our times, Dr. Martin Luther King."

"Dr. King, yeah?"

"Yes, brother, they were all young, and in my opinion, all chosen, and with their divinely inspired deeds they changed the course of history and the world."

Big John nodding his head in total agreement. "Yes, Doc, history was truly made on August 28, 2008, when BARACK OBAMA became the first black man ever nominated by a major party to the office of American presidency."

"Call it prophecy! Call it prediction! It was all in the dreamers' dreams, brother."

"Dreams, just like in Dr. King's famous 'I Have a Dream' speech forty-something years ago. Amazing!"

"Yes, brother. And we are now in the year of our Lord 2008, and November 4 is just a breath away. Has it been forty years since? You do the math."

"What do you mean forty years?"

"The very year and time dreamed, prophesied, and even predicted by RFK."

Big John took a deep breath and exhaling loudly said, "So, BARACK OBAMA is the very one. He is the black Messiah then, he is."

"That's what some people think."

"But you sound like you don't think he is, Doc? If OBAMA is not the Messiah, who then do you think he is?"

I thought about the question for a few seconds and said, "You know, somebody asked me the same question a few weeks ago."

"And?"

"BARACK OBAMA, in my opinion, is no black Messiah. But he is special." I took my last sip from my teacup and said, "OBAMA is a special kind of a man. He is here, flesh and blood, just like you and I. Now watch this, BARACK OBAMA, phenomenon, brother, is the wakeup call, a vessel, to help liberate the inherent messiah, the native goodness in us all."

"Very brilliant, Doc," Big John said in a rather loud voice. "Very brilliant. I could never have thought of it in that way."

"That's what the OBAMA phenomenon is all about, Big John, and again, that's just my opinion."

"Your opinion, Doc," said Big John, "is indeed a goldmine."

"But let us not be fooled, though, because this is still America."

"Yes?"

"There are still elements of the American Social Sect out there, ranting and begrudging the blazing 'Change-Movement' of these times you know. And would do everything in their malicious powers to stop the movement."

"Of course there are," agreed Big John, sitting up straight. "The clan and their surrogates are still a dark evil-force in our society no doubt"

"To those kind of people, I say, relax my friends, there is no sane real to bear hate as armor. Take a very deep breath and exhale."

"But Doc," Big John asks, "now how can such breathing exercises cure hate and stuff?"

I smiled and said, "Try this simple exercise yourself three times for three days. It is good therapy for your heart and any enraged nerves that may exist, I grant you that."

"But Doc, we are not talking about me. It's those serpents and their guileful acts that I'm worried about."

"Okay, brother, you are right. Now to those elements of our society still un-repenting and unforgiving, still possessed by an unrelenting antipathy toward OBAMA, toward *change*? No problem. This I say to them, and please, Big John, put this in bold print: "Do the world a favor and get out of the way, or kindly take our Lord Jesus Christ's advice, rightfully stated in the book of Mathew, chapter 6, verses 43-48 (for Christians only)."

Big John took another deep breath and exhaled. "You can be hard hitting, Doc, I swear."

"Please don't get me wrong. I am in no way advocating a monotonous 'my way or no way' module or system. No, never. This is still America. The land of the free. The land that accords the freedom to speak our minds and choose our favorite president. For that is written in stone."

"Huzzah!" Big John exclaimed.

"But what is not and should not be encouraged or tolerated by any degree is the freedom to harm. Especially the very one, or others, who have nothing but good will for the human race, all human race. For thereunto I say to you, borrowing an excerpt from the Book of the Gospels, 'For it were better,' Jesus Christ forewarned, 'that such person (of heinous predisposition) was never born.'"

I got up from my chair, reached into my pocket, and pulled out a couple of Ricola drops. I unwrapped one and after putting it into my mouth said, "Would you like a Ricola drop, Big John?

"Sure, Doc," he replied, stuffing his notepad into his briefcase. Big John took the Ricola off my right palm and quickly unwrapped it.

He dropped the Ricola into his mouth and said: "Hmmm, this will sure drown all them garlic and the onions."

"Watch out, now," I said, "that's no Certs, Big John, and in no way a prescription to go kissing any girl on your way home."

Big John stood at attention and raised his right hand as if standing front of a judge and said, with an un-genuine face, "I swear by my wife's big lips."

I smiled and said to myself, "Well, I've never met Big John's wife, but if her lips are as he swears (just like my wife's big and sensuously inviting parts), Big John has no reason on earth to hunger for another (woman's) lips." So I gave him the benefit of doubt. "Sure!"

As we exited the restaurant door, he stretched out his right hand to me and said, "Thank you, Doc, for everything. You've given me a lot to chew on."

"What, you're a Capricorn too? No, I was just joking, Big John."

"As a matter of fact," replied Big John, shaking my hand spiritedly, "I am indeed. January 15, just like Dr. Martin Luther King."

For a few seconds, I was agape and out of words as I stared at his big face from my heightened angle.

Big John quickly withdrew his hand from mine and said, "Doc, why are you looking at me as if you've suddenly seen a ghost?"

I shook my head, a-smiling. "Big John, you are my brother indeed. We both have the same birth date."

"Amazing!" Big John exclaimed, wrapping his large arms around me with all his heart. "Good Lord, I've always suspected there was something special about you, I mean between us, and who knows, my grandfathers may have roots in Igbo-land too."

"That may not surprise me," I muttered. In my opinion, most black people in America came from the west coast of Africa." After he let go of me, I took a very deep breath and said, "Now that I know that you and I are of the same soul origin, let's get together like family and do something. Maybe travel to Africa someday."

"Doc, that has always been my dream."

"And with a little help brother John," I added, reaching for door keys, "dreams do come true."

Big John nodded beamingly. "I vote yes, Brother," he said, raising his right fist in the air before opening his car door.

# Part 2

November 3, a day before America went to the polling booths to finally select their new president, the day before the long-awaited Tuesday, a different kind of news came to BARACK very early that morning. Mrs. Madelyn Dunham, the very woman who raised him, his "Toot," had died.

Imagine. Just, imagine.

Two weeks earlier, though, it had been reported on CNN and other news media that OBAMA had taken time off from his presidential campaign to visit his then ailing grandma in Hawaii. The meeting of the grandma and her beloved grandson (from Thursday through Friday) was exclusively private and we now know their last physical meeting on earth.

While in Hawaii, his wife, Michelle, and Senator Clinton (a former rival), kept his "Hope and Change" message alive on the campaign trail.

Seeing and listening to Michelle speak at a rally hosted by CU students at the Boulder Campus, I came to this profound realization. I concluded without any doubt in my mind that America cannot ask for a better and more competent couple in the White House at this point in time. Yes, Michelle and her insightfully gifted husband do get it. Yes they do.

I also have to admit that seeing my own son (who is a senior at CU) amongst the many enthused young men standing gallantly behind Mrs. OBAMA as she addressed the student crowd made me proud and drew me closer to the OBAMAS.

When BARACK finally emerged from Toot's house in Hawaii that Friday morning, he looked different. He seemed stoic, calm, and as tempered as a windless sea.

But the next day, back in the campaign thereafter, as he plowed into the last and decisive phase of the marathon campaign, BARACK OBAMA is seen standing as tall as ever, undaunted, animated, and seemingly much more inspiring. And did I say marathon? Well, isn't his father a Kenyan? The land of elite marathoners like George Nchoro, Rose Jebet, Samuel Wanjiru, and John Ngugi, to mention a few?

I submit to you, my friends, that BARACK OBAMA has that unique gene in him. He evidently has the steps, the drive, the thoroughbred enduring stamina, and the passion. Political marathon passion, that is.

Masterfully and mightily endowed, BARACK OBAMA.

In the campaign arena, OBAMA is as ever, issue focused, and in every step steadfast in his message for hope and change. With shoulders high and seemingly winged like an eagle, you can't help but wonder and ask yourself, "Who is this man, really, that stands so tall and strong even in face of all odds, especially with such personal calamity at his doorstep? How many hundreds or thousands of invisible angels, one wonders, are beside this young man, winging him on? Huh?"

It is not surprising, then, that many, I mean many, folks who have been inspired beyond their imaginations are now calling BARACK OBAMA the 'Messiah'?"

BARACK OBAMA, a Messiah? The long-awaited savior and deliverer?

In my opinion? No, I think not. And neither does he.

Although OBAMA has appeared on the political stage with the voice and looks of an elite rock star and has singlehandedly shaken the pillars of a long-established cultural and political fabric of the American society, and thereby provoking an unprecedented social consciousness, he is no Messiah. And he strongly declines any such messianic personification.

OBAMA, I think, is just a phenomenon of the times, the phenomenon of change.

The phenomenon and aptly a placatory vessel, to atone for the past, as well as these extraordinary times.

OBAMA is the vessel for change. The change we must have. With change, we can overcome the gloom of our bedeviled past, pledge, and plough the highway to peace and prosperity!

OBAMA is the vessel by which the dreamers' dream is about to be realized.

He is the vessel (in accordance with Dr. Martin Luther King's dream) by which America has finally risen up and lived the true meaning of its creed: that "all men are created equal."

The OBAMA phenomenon is the vehicle that has arrived. It has arrived to drive and bring the quiet Messiah, the humanity and goodness native in all mankind, out of you and me. Yes, that Messiah (good Lord) is in me as it is in you.

So, if there is one thing, just one thing, that BARACK OBAMA said as he crisscrossed the entire landscape of America, that touched your heart deeply and caused you to get off your couch and go vote for the first time in your adult life, well, therein is the Messiah in you, in function.

If there was one thing BARACK OBAMA said or did to help you really understand the issue at stake, well, thereupon is your Messiah, rekindled.

If there was one thing BARACK OBAMA said or did that made you call up your neighbors and help them go forth and vote, that is the Messiah in you, at work.

And finally, my fellow Americans, if there was one thing BARACK OBAMA said or did that made you feel and or do a good thing, even for one day, a-ha, you are therefore in part a driving force of the universal Messiah. The energy of the present, with her inherent formidable force for change, is the Messiah-ship in the OBAMA phenomenon.


*Tuesday, November 4, 2008*

This day will forever be remembered.

I woke up earlier than usual. As part of my routine these days, I turned on my personal computer to check my e-mail. There were over fifty new e-mail messages in my inbox despite the fact that I'd checked and emptied it the night before. Most of the e-mail was about the election. Vote! Vote! Vote! I had sent and forwarded election information to many of my friends and associates, including reminders to vote early. As for me, after listening to OBAMA stress the importance of early voting, I took advantage of our state's mail-in voting opportunity early. I even called the county election commission office to make sure my vote has been received. It was.

My daughter and son, who were voting for the first time, were already part of the "Rock the Vote" thing, they were all over OBAMA.

There were also e-mails from several candidates making their final campaign pitch. How these people got my name and e-mail address, I have no idea; nevertheless, such sociopolitical recognition made me feel special and important, to say the least.

But there was this message that was looking for volunteers. "African American women for change," the caption said.

I wrote the number down on a piece of paper, and after expunging the rest of my junk e-mail, I turned off the computer and went to say "good morning" to my bathroom mirror. I did other things too, like brushing my teeth, shaving, and of course showering. You see, in my house, getting a hot shower depends on who wakes up first and who is first to jump in behind the shower curtain. This morning, with my wife still at work at the hospital (having been called in for an all night shift), I really enjoyed a very long hot shower today. Yeah!

It was about 8:55 a.m. when I called the contact number for the volunteer job. Without bothering to ask or investigate what the change was for, I asked if I could volunteer in their movement (you know, as a man). The lady at the other end of the phone line was excited to hear my voice. "Please come and join us, brother," she cried, "and bring your friends if you can."

Their office was located on north Washington Street in the Five Point neighborhood.

I then called my wife. Crazy in her thoughts at times, but I love her dearly.

She still thinks about the OBAMA-Mama Dance with Ellen DeGeneres, that it was the most exciting thing on TV.

Not trusting the mail-in ballot thing, my wife took advantage of the early voting also. She voted five days ago.

"What are you gonna do with your patients today?" she asked as she was getting into her car, chewing something.

"Babe, my patients are very understanding, I grant you that. I will go to the office right away and call them."

"Okay, babe." She paused, probably swallowing something. "But make sure you get home before things get crazy out there, you know what I mean."

"Babe, come rain, come sun, 'Go, OBAMA, go! We both chanted and then hung up.'"

I arrived at exactly 11 a.m., surprising myself too, but at what turned up to be the wrong building. You see, the Hendell building is a very popular place in Five Points, with a lot of business offices, including the Center for African-American Leadership, of which I was part for about two years. I assumed (without writing the correct address down before I left my house) this was the meeting place. Sister Joyce was her charming self this morning at the bar, serving and entertaining six guests before I took my seat.

She quickly recognized me. "Hi, Dr. O," she greeted smilingly, all eyes turned toward my seat. "I haven't seen you for a long time."

"Good morning, Sister Joyce," I replied, taking my fall jacket off my shoulders. "I moved back to Aurora almost two years now, you know, especially since they stopped our TV program."

"It's a real shame, Dr. O. I used to enjoy watching you on TV, talking about black health. Especially the point you made on one of your shows about 'thrifty gene.' Man, that really hit home. It made me change most of my eating habits, I swear."

"What's the titty gene?" asked one of the guys at the far left side, downing half the contents of his glass. "I sure would like to have me one of those."

"Be quiet, Archie," Sister Joyce cut in. "It is called the 'thrifty gene,' titty-head. Your skinny legs don't have to worry about that kind of gene, if you ask me."

Meanwhile, the front door flipped open, and I turned to see if the lady I was looking for had arrived. It was yet another middle-aged guy in long winter coat, shuffling in.

"By the way, Dr. O," continued Sister Joyce, "all the drinks and snacks are on the house today, so please help yourself."

"Wow!" I said. "Do you have any hot tea?"

"Sure, Dr. O," she replied. She grabbed a black tea cup in one hand and gingerly filled it with hot water, and with the other hand she picked up a small tray of teabags.

"Which blend would you like? I have orange, peppermint, and green tea."

"Green tea is good, Sister Joyce," I replied gratefully. She placed the tea bag on a small paper towel next to my cup.

"Sugar or cream?"

"No thank you," I replied. "I drink my tea straight."

Presently, Archie, the one Sister Joyce called 'titty-head,' was standing beside me with an open folder. He pulled a flyer out and, placing it in front of me, asked, "Did you get one of these, Doc?"

I glanced through the headline: "A hundred Black Men Cook-a-thon."

"No, I sure didn't," I replied.

"Well, that's what we are trying to organize today," explained Archie. "Glad you can join us."

"I am here to volunteer for the 'OBAMA for Change' ad I saw in my e-mail. I spoke with a lady this morning. Her name is Pat."

Everybody looked at each other. "I don't know no Pat doing anything here," said Archie. "Do you know Pat Sister Joyce?"

"I sure don't," replied Sister Joyce, equally perplexed. "No such event going on here this early that I know of, Doc." Then she added, "Maybe you should try the Plaza at Twenty-Sixth and Welton."

"The lady said they were at Twenty-Fourth and Washington, so I assumed it must be in this building."

"There will be a mighty celebration here tonight for sure," said Sister Joyce. "I'm hoping and praying to God we celebrate, for a change."

"I drink to that," shouted the guys in one accord.

I stood up and put on my jacket and said, "Well, folks, I'm gonna drive up to the plaza now. Thank you, Sister Joyce, for the tea."

"You are very welcome, Dr. O," she replied with a wink in her left eye. "You can always come back and have another cup of tea on me."

I smiled at her and headed toward the front double glass door. Before exiting, I overheard Archie or one of the other guys snickering at Sister Joyce for trying to flirt with the doctor. Flirting? Not by my reckoning. As long as I've known Sister Joyce, she had been that kind of a pleasant individual that makes good company. I guess some shallow-minded men could mistake her friendliness for flirting, but I don't really care. Not at this moment, I have a lot on my mind and beating myself up for getting my information so wrong this morning.

"The plaza is on Twenty-Sixth, not on Twenty-Fourth," I pondered as I started my car, "and I can swear that lady Pat said Twenty-Fourth. Hmm, this doesn't make sense."

At the stop sign at Twenty-Fourth, I turned right, north, onto Washington street, taking it easy on my gas pedal, as I glanced from left to right, looking for some sort of sign.

As I pulled to a stop at the corner of Twenty-Fifth and Washington, I looked right and saw a sign on the window of an old two-story brick building second from the corner. It read, "African-American Women for Change."

A-ha! I took a deep breath and exhaled with a loud puff.

There was no car behind me at this time, so I backed up a few yards, pulled right in front of the building, and parked.

The long wooden door was wide open, so I let myself in.

"You must be Ellie, right?" I greeted the pleasant looking young lady with her right hand stretched toward me.

"I sure am," I replied, grabbing her palm in mine. It was very warm and soft. "And you must be Pat, the director?"

"Yes, indeed," she replied with zest and immediately took me around the long oval table, introducing me to the rest of the young ladies (five altogether), some sitting, others standing, but all busy, sorting and putting campaign flyers together.

"That is Yemi," she said, pointing to an eight-year-old boy in the adjoining room. "Yemi, come and say hi to Ellie," she ordered him.

The boy dropped his backpack on a small table and rolled (on his wheeled tennis shoes) toward me.

"Hi," the little boy greeted, and without waiting for my response, he spun around on his shoes, rolling back to the room where his backpack was.

Presently, an elderly lady, who Pat introduced to me as the Matron, arrived with yet another box load of flyers. She and one of the young workers (or maybe a volunteer too) stayed in the office, while we, all wearing our "Change" T-shirts, including young Yemi, left for our point of operation in two cars only. Yemi and me rode with Pat. The other four ladies followed right behind us in a silver Toyota sedan.

I later found out as we drove toward downtown in Pat's raggedy Mazda that Yemi's father is Nigerian (no surprise there) and that "that fool (as she jokingly referred to him) "would not sign our divorce papers." That was a little surprising. Then she turns her head to me, with her right hand now off the steering wheel and arched to her hip, and asks, "Ellie, are African men that strong headed, like my ex?"

African men? Africa? Man, I pulled my lower lip tight and shrugged my shoulders.

Trying to deflect and change such a loaded topic, I tactically swung my head backward and said to her son, sited in the left corner of the overstuffed back seat, "It looks like Yemi boy came home early from school today?"

"No, sir," interjected Pat. "We don't go to school or work on Election Day. It's a family tradition."

"Wow, such is a very noble tradition, Pat," I commended. "You should call your Congressman—"

"Or woman."

"Yyyes! And have them pass a bill making Election Day a federal holiday."

"Now you're talking," she cheered. "I'll vote for that."

It was in the middle of lunchtime when we finally arrived at our point of operation (after parking the cars in a two-hour-metered parking zone area). It spanned Lincoln Street at the West end of the Capitol to Broadway off Colfax Avenue. While the other girls took their sign-waving posts at various positions within the operating parameters, I helped Pat erect an eight-foot mobile billboard with preprinted campaign ads.

Amongst our freebies were "African-American Women for Change" T-shirts and flags, "Yes, We Can" T-shirts, flags, and OBAMA buttons.

And man, I needn't say anything at all but wave the flag in my right hand and raise the placard in my left high, and passersby on foot and in their cars would shout, yell, and honk: "Go, OBAMA. Go, OBAMA." Even young Yemi was into the act, waving his OBAMA flag with his right hand and breaking every now and then to give away an OBAMA pin, as he masterfully rolled on his wheeled, flashing tennis shoes between Lincoln street and Broadway on the south sidewalk of Colfax Avenue. What an amazing youngster, Yemi-boy.

"Pardon me, sir," said this one lady and her friend (both in their mid—to late twenties) in heavily-accented English, "can I take a picture of you with the big sign?" She pointed to the billboard Pat and I had just mounted.

"Sure," I replied, grinning to my ears as I held the edge of the eight-foot billboard in one hand and my "OBAMA for Change" flag in the other hand. She snapped twice, and so did her companion.

Out of curiosity, I asked their nationality.

"We come from the Netherlands," replied the more fluent partner, while the other, either shy or weak in the English language, just smiled. "We come with other peoples to many American cities," she continued, "to witness the election."

"Amazing. People coming from all over the world to witness this election?"

"Yes, I like OBAMA very much," professed the one talking, while the other nodded her head as she giggled in apparent agreement. I gave them T-shirts and two OBAMA buttons. They were delighted. Even the one that never uttered a word said, "Thank you" twice as she carefully stuffed her souvenirs in her large backpack.

I was pleasantly surprised at Pat's style and ardor. With placard and flag in her hands, she sang, danced, and even displayed some acrobatic feats. It appeared to me, watching how natural and conversant she was with the locals—some pedestrians, some on bikes, even calling them by their first names, and vice versa as they traversed Colfax Avenue—that Pat must have been once a street girl herself, or just street smart. There were at least three guys she knew enough to make them postpone their own daily agenda for the moment and join in our fun sign-waving enterprise. Exciting.

There were some rare moments, though, when I noticed that a driver, waiting at the stoplight at Colfax and Lincoln, would not look my way, even as I waved and flashed my smiling "OBAMA" placards at him. I observed him grinding his teeth so hard, praying for the "damn light" to change so he could speed the hell away from me. I could easily surmise that he too was one of the few unrepentant Republicans left. For such travelers, I paused for a few seconds and prayed. I sincerely prayed for their safe journey home before the election results started buzzing in.

At 5:30 p.m., we dismantled our post at the southwest corner of Colfax and Lincoln Avenue. We collected what was left and took them back into the trunk of Pat's Mazda, parked two and half blocks away.

"Thank you, Pat," I said as we navigated our way back to the office.

"No, dude," Pat replied, patting my left thigh. "I should be thanking you. It is a great honor having someone of your class come join our cause. I owe you man."

"I mean it, Pat. This is the most fun job I have ever in all of my adult life, without pay."

"Yes, you will be paid, Ellie," replied Pat. "Just fill out the worksheet when we get back to the office."

I shook my head. "No Pat, this is part of my investment for an OBAMA presidency."

"Mr. Ellie," Yemi called from his back seat, "can I ask you a personal question?"

"Please, Yemi, ask me any question," I replied, turning my curious ears toward him.

"Did you vote for OBAMA?"

"Not necessary, Yemi. I voted for Sasha and the children of the world."

"Sasha?" Pat cut in. "She is not even on the ballot."

"Mom, who is Sasha?

"She is one of BARACK OBAMA'S kids, babe."

"Oh, thank you, Mom." Yemi exhales. "I think I get it now."

I turned to Pat, who seemed perplexed at her eight-year-old son's paradoxical deduction, and said, "You see, he gets it. I grant you this, Pat. Your son could one day grow up to run for president, just like BARACK OBAMA."

Pat went quiet for a few seconds. Just as we were about to pull in front of her office, she stopped in the middle of the road, looked at me, and said, "Ellie, you are different. I swear you are either a prophet or some Messiah."

I shook my head. "I am neither," I replied.

"You are then fricken strange, man, and I like strange and crazy men." She let out a big smile.

"Pat, this might surprise you, but we have in us all a Messiah in disguise."

She backed into an open space in front of the office building and parked. Yemi opened the back passenger door and jumped out. Before I could open my door, she pulled on my left arm and said, "Ellie."

"Yes, Pat," I replied, a little surprised.

She leaned her head toward me, for a kiss, I thought, but instead said in a whisper, "Listen, this is off record, and don't think I am fricken crazy either, because I am not."

"Okay." I'm dying to hear what the secret is.

"I am really a closet Ralph Nader supporter."

My whole body went numb for a second or two.

"You are—"

"Shhhhh," she cut in, placing her forefinger over her lips. "I trust you enough now to really let you in one of my little idiosyncrasies. So that's between you and me. Now let's go eat. I am starving." I obliged.

Inside the office, the matron and her assistant had cleared the long oval table of all papers, flyers, and campaign signs. In their place were trays of assorted cheeses, breads, meats, salads, chips, and soft drinks.

I made myself a moderate sized chicken sandwich and grabbed a bottle of water, but before I left I stepped over to the adjoining room to bid little Yemi good-bye. Yemi, already engrossed in his computer game, was oblivious to my presence.

"Bye, Yemi," I said from about two feet away from his desk.

"Oh, Mr. Ellie." Yemi jolted in his chair. "You almost scared me."

"I am sorry Yemi-boy, I just came to say bye and wish you well in your schooling."

"Thank you, Mr. Ellie," Yemi replied absentmindedly.

"Got you. Oh yes, I got you, babe. Five hundred points, yeah! And Yemi actually made an "I got you" sign with his little fists.

You see, one thing I personally learned from my own son is never to bother a young kid (especially a boy) with a civics lecture when he is 99.9 percent into his computer game world. I slowly stepped away from his field of operation and met his mom, Pat, halfway toward the front door.

Almost immediately, I heard my name. "Mr. Ellie, bye, Mr. Ellie," Yemi shouted, at the top of his voice. "And thank you for helping my mom today. You are a very nice man, Mr. Ellie."

"You are a very good boy, Yemi-boy," I replied in an equally high tone. "Thank you and good-bye."

Pat's livened, maternal eyes and mine met in acquiescence. "You are a special kind of guy," Pat said to me as we walked to the front door. "Again, thanks for everything."

"It's an honor, Pat, to be part of a noble cause. I really had a lot of fun today."

"And when this is allllll over," she replied, a-yawning, "I'll give you a call."

"Please do."

She stretched out her right hand to me, I grabbed it, and before I let go, she asked, "Do you think OBAMA has a good chance to be our next president?"

She let out a wry smile. "I give him a gooood 54 percent."

"And what percentage would you give Ralph Nader?"

She quickly pulled her hand away from my grip and almost simultaneously placed the forefinger of her right hand across her suddenly tightened lips.

I nodded with a grin. She waved me bye-bye.

Fifty-four percent.

That is a very good percentage, if you ask me, considering how far OBAMA has had to go. Really. As I headed home (eastbound on Colfax Ave) on this beautiful Tuesday afternoon, no snow in the forecast, just an evening breeze that make your head think it's the last day of spring, I still noticed a lot of campaign flag wavers, just like I did, at almost every major intersection. Pat's 54 percent prediction was about 5 percent lower than my own 59 percent estimation. I came to my summation by noting and (mentally) tallying the number of drivers that honked, cheered, or had OBAMA sign on their cars and trucks; and by how many pedestrians gave us a high-five sign or stopped to get an OBAMA T-shirt and or a 'Yes We Can' flag. It was my opinion that if such a trend was in place at every major street corner in all the cities of the United States, victory would be ringing in the OBAMA house before midnight.

But Ralph Nader? Pat, a closet supporter of Ralph Nader? Impossible.

How can this strong and energetic young lady wake up every day for the last six months or so, working tirelessly for the election one man and at the same time a closet supporter of another candidate? Huh?

I could only shake my head, hoping for one second that Pat was joking. But she was not, and according to her, she is not crazy either.

Although, in my judgment, Pat would not qualify as having a dual personality, it's still a baffling phenomenon, and I hope not a normal finding amongst voters across the nation.

When I returned home, I could hear the sound of our TV from the garage. As I opened the front door, I saw Ike, his American wife Mary, and Iffie, his newly arrived immigrant cousin, all seated in the parlor, eating goat meat soup (my wife's favorite dish), and at the same time, with their eyes, I fixated nervously on our new plasma TV screen my son had just bought us a few months ago (for our twenty-sixth wedding anniversary). Thanks a bunch.

"I was wondering when you were gonna make it home," my wife cried from the kitchen.

"Good morning, everybody" I greeted, stepping over to the kitchen to give her a kiss.

"It sure smells pleasantly delicious in this house. Hm-hm-hm."

She gave me a sexy bump with her hips and said, "Well, babe, if you take off your jacket and go sit down, I'll bring you a plate."

"My friend," Ike cut in after a sip of his drink, "tell me this: when is it not good morning in your big coconut head?"

"Brother Ike, I'm glad you asked that," I replied, walking over to his chair and grabbing his right hand in a warm (hand) shake. "My answer is never!"

I patted his wife, Mary, on the shoulder, and then turned toward Iffie, who quickly glanced at her wrist watch and then at the wall clock behind the TV and said, "But, Brother Ellie, it's almost 6 p.m. now."

"Really? I grinned as I took my fall jacket off my back and proceeded to hang it in the living room closet. "Sister Iffie, I pray, don't let them man-made tick tocks we call the clock fool you. The only ticker that I pay attention to is the one in my heart—I mean my head—and it always says, 'Good morning', because it reminds me to be thankful for getting to see another day."

Iffie busted out laughing and fanned her open lips at the same time. "Brother Ellie we know you always say 'Good Morning' regardless of the time," she chuckled, sniffing as she rushed over to the kitchen with her now empty glass, "always something else, I swear."

"Yeah, sister. You better drink more cool water," I said loudly. "My wife always makes her food hot and spicy, you know." And then in a rather lower voice I added, "Just like her, hot and spicy."

"Ohhhhhhhhhh," crooned Ike. "Sister Di, did you hear what your husband just said? Watch out now."

"What did he say? I can't hear," she yelled from the kitchen, the vent fan, apparently on high.

"Shhhhhh," hushed Mary, Ike's wife. "Guys, can we hear what the announcer is saying please?"

You see, Mary is a die-hard OBAMA supporter. She is white and works for the Aurora public schools. Surprisingly, Mary loves spicy food, especially the way Di makes it. And like myself, she too has both an OBAMA T-shirt and a button on this evening.

"You're right, sister, I apologize." I then sat down in my massage chair but did not press the button to turn it on.

"So is any result in yet?"

"Not yet," replied Mary, who is more into political details than her husband. "It seems like Colorado might be going from a swing state to a blue state according to recent polls. From all I've seen today, I say, 'Yes we can.'"

That immediately brought Ike to the floor, dancing and singing, "Yes we can. Yes we can. Yes we can. Lady Di, please give me another bottle of beer. Yes we can. Mary, my darling, you're driving home tonight."

"Yes, I will," replied Mary laconically. And then she added, "Now, James Brown impersonator, please get back to your seat and stop celebrating before it's time."

My wife was at her pleasant best tonight, cooking and serving with zest and pleasure. She made sure everybody had enough to eat and drink before she finally made a plate for herself and took her seat beside Iffie.

As for me, I took over the remote control, flipping it in between bites of my meal from CNN to CNBC. At some lengthy commercial intervals, I even checked out the spin on FOX.

The early results in a few southern states made my stomach churn to the point that I stopped eating.

"Those are redneck states," commented Mary. "They would never vote Democrat, let alone for a black man. No, we don't worry about those anyway."

While Mary's explanation might have been true, that still didn't help calm my shaky fingers at this point in time. Several times my table spoon missed the mouth it was meant to feed, dripping and spilling hot soup all over my sweatshirt. Nor did I blame the spoon for falling off my shaky finger either. There was at this point an obvious disconnect between this special metal, me, and my present temperament. And yet, for some crazy reason, the spoon always fell right into my soup bowl. Gee whiz.

I guess this uncanny ritual went on and on, till I heard Mary yelling and shouting, at about 8 p.m. Denver time.

"Yeah! Yeah!" shouted Mary, getting out of her seat for the first time since the results started coming in. "We finally won in Ohio, and now Colorado has gone for OBAMA too. Hurray! Hurray!"

I quickly flipped the remote from CNN to CNBC. It is true. We have won Ohio, and Colorado too, by 54 percent, just like Pat had predicted. Amazing.

Presently, a few more results trickled in from the northern states, and minute by minute, electoral votes keep on heaping in OBAMA'S column. Like magic, my hands, heart, stomach, and me became one intrepid whole. Fear no more. CNN, CNBC, FOX, ABC, CBS, and NBC all became convinced that a mighty political shift—of a seismic caliber—had happened in America.

BARACK OBAMA, an African American, is the next president of the United States. Huzzah! Huzzah! Huzzah!

I danced, we danced, we sang, we prayed, we cried and cried, we hoorayed and we daaaaaaaaaaanced.

BARACK OBAMA has exceeded all expectations.

Yes, Americans have spoken. BARACK OBAMA, a black man, has been elected president. The forty-fourth president of the United States is a black man. Finally.

So, rejoice America, rejoice. Rejoice, for the change we need is come.

Rejoice, Children of America, of the world, rejoice. Rejoice, for the future is brilliant.

Rejoice, all ye who have been oppressed, suppressed, and displaced, rejoice. Rejoice, for opportunity and parity abound.

Rejoice, all ye hardworking people, rejoice. Rejoice, for ye shall rightfully inherit the fruit of your labor.

Rejoice for education, please join me, rejoice. Rejoice, for the limit of progress and enlightenment is in the high heavens.

Rejoice for healthcare, rejoice. Rejoice, for healthcare for all citizens is finally a humane act that is so right.

Rejoice for prosperity, rejoice. Rejoice, for the gloom and doom of the Bush era shall be erased by the booms that change can right.

Rejoice for unity, America rejoice. Rejoice, for the advocate and embodiment of unity is the chosen one.

Rejoice for peace, all the people of the world, rejoice. Rejoice, for BARACK OBAMA, a friend and prime proponent of strength through peace and understanding, is now the president.

Let all hearts rejoice, from the northernmost barrow of Alaska to the southernmost keys of Florida and Naalehu, Hawaii. Let all hearts rejoice, from the city of Lubec, Maine, to Ozette, Washington, let our hearts rejoice. Yeah, let Lebanon, Kansas, rejoice, the Center-web of the Great USA, Aha! Let all souls, here and beyond, in one accord, share and relish the fulfillment of the dreams of our founding fathers, and all advocates of their dreams for parity and justice for all. Yes, at last, the dreamers' dream. Huzzah!

# Dedication

To my late father, Johnson Ezemuru Onyeali, who on that early Monday morning (I had just turned seven), taught me that when faced with a challenge (in this particular case, clearing our overgrown farmland and readying it for the planting season), doing something is more fruitful than doing nothing.

"Son, give me your cutlass," he said, "and let me show you how with one strike of the blade at a time, you can bring all this forest down before your scared eyes." After clearing the ambient brush, my father gave me back my cutlass and said, "Now, son, you can do it." I have never been scared of the forest since.

To my late uncle, Mathias Chimezie Onyeali, who took me under his wing (after my father's death) and raised me up as his own.

To my late aunt, Nkika-Rachel Emenyonu (nee, Onyeali), who taught me by the example of her own personal achievements, defying all cultural odds after her husband's death, that standing your ground, hard work, and assertiveness are three primary virtues to success.

To my late grandmother Utoro-Fanny Durugo (nee, Anumodu), who, overjoyed at the birth of her first grandson, showered me with love as I grew up.

# About the Author

Dr. Eleazar Azuoma Onyeali was born in Umunjam, a little village north of Owerri Township (now capital of Imo state) of Nigeria. Like most of his peers of the time on the Biafra side, he was caught in the Nigerian-Biafran civil war crossfire (1967-1970). As war raged on, he spent most of his late teens, and later his young adult life, hiding in refugee camps. The third year into the war, he was conscripted into the Biafra army and was on the verge of being shipped to the warfront a few months later when their leader, Commander O. Ojukwu, finally surrendered to the overwhelming military might of the federal government.

At the end of the hostilities (thank God), Eleazar traveled to the United States to continue his education, which had been interrupted by the bloody unrest. Eleazar was going to school in Chicago, but two years was all he could take, the city was too rough, too cold. At the end of his second year, he transferred from Loop Junior College in Chicago to Metropolitan State College in Denver, Colorado. Eleazar found the weather in Denver to be much more tolerable than what he experienced in Chicago, so he decided to stay.

Eleazar obtained his Bachelor of Science from Metropolitan State College in Denver, but it would be twelve years later (after discovering and developing a keen interest in the field of chiropractic natural healthcare) that he decided to pursue a career in chiropractic. He received his doctorate in chiropractic four years later from Life University School of Chiropractic, Marietta, Georgia.

Upon graduation, Eleazar returned to Denver to reunite with his wife and two children.

Dr. Onyeali has been practicing for ten years now in Aurora, Colorado, and is a frequent contributor (on health related issues) to the *Body of Christ News*, a local Denver newspaper.